THE PATH TO PERSONAL POWER

THE PATH TO PERSONAL POWER

Napoleon Hill

Published by

PRABHAT PRAKASHAN PVT. LTD.
4/19 Asaf Ali Road,
New Delhi-110002 (INDIA)
e-mail: prabhatbooks@gmail.com

ISBN 978-93-5266-438-2

THE PATH TO PERSONAL POWER
by Napoleon Hill

Edition
2025

Price
₹ 350 (Rupees Three Hundred Fifty Only)

Printed at
S.S. Japan Arts, Delhi

Foreword

By Don M. Green,
Executive Director, The Napoleon Hill Foundation

As a young reporter working for *Bob Taylor's Magazine* in 1908, Napoleon Hill conducted his first major interview at the home of steel magnate Andrew Carnegie. As many followers of Napoleon Hill's life and writings know, Carnegie asked young Napoleon to spend the next twenty years or so, without pay, conducting interviews so that he could write the first book in America on how its great men had achieved success.

Napoleon accepted the challenge, did the necessary research and interviews, and produced the first major treatise on the science of personal achievement. Published in 1928 as *Law of Success*, it was followed in 1937 by an abbreviated version, titled *Think and Grow Rich*, which is without a doubt the most read and most-valued motivational book of the 20th century, and thereafter.

The Napoleon Hill Foundation, founded by Mr. Hill in 1962, eight years before his death, continues to promote his philosophy. It has licensed his books in over fifty languages throughout the world. It is a non-profit charitable foundation which uses its revenues to endow scholarships, teach Hill's principles in correctional institutions, and conduct research into his life and work. It has recently unearthed three unpublished full-length books by Mr. Hill, one of which, *Outwitting the Devil*, was published in 2011 to critical acclaim.

The book you are about to read is excerpted from a series of lessons on success that Napoleon Hill wrote in 1941 at the urging of Dr. William Plumer Jacobs of Clinton, South Carolina. Dr. Jacobs was President of Presbyterian College, owner of Jacobs Press, and consultant to many textile mill owners. He had heard Mr. Hill lecture a year earlier, was impressed, and believed that a self-help course and lecture series by Mr. Hill would help South Carolina and its neighbouring states emerge from the lingering effects of the Great Depression. Believing that many Americans were still beaten down by the hard times of the 1930s, and were depending too much on the government for economic support, Mr. Hill saw this opportunity to teach people how to succeed.

Napoleon accepted Dr. Jacobs' offer and moved to Clinton to write his lessons on success. He called the lessons "Mental Dynamite," taking the title from an observation Mr. Carnegie made when they first met: "The power with which we think is mental dynamite." He authored seventeen lessons, in booklet format, and each based on one of the principles of success he had discovered in his discussions with Mr. Carnegie and other men of achievement. Most of the lessons included lengthy excerpts from Napoleon's interviews with Mr. Carnegie, and then set forth specific examples of how Mr. Carnegie's principles had been applied by other successful people in America.

Mr. Hill's Mental Dynamite booklets and lecture series were well received, but everything changed on December 7 of the year of their publication, when Japan bombed Pearl Harbour and the United States entered World War II. These Mental Dynamite lessons were put aside during the war, and largely forgotten thereafter. In this book, the Foundation has put together three of the lessons, which focus on what many people think are the most important of all of Hill and Carnegie's principles.

The Mental Dynamite lessons chosen for this book are those that anyone can use to achieve personal power. More importantly, they must be used in order to achieve personal power. The principles are Definiteness of Purpose, the Mastermind Principle, and Going the Extra Mile. As these lessons from the Foundation's archives are read, and more importantly applied, you will begin your journey on the path to personal power.

Think!

Croesus, a wise philosopher and confidential advisor to Cyrus, king of the Persians, said:

"I am reminded, O king, that
there is a Wheel on which
the affairs of men revolve,
and its mechanism is such
that it prevents any man
from being always fortunate."

There is a Wheel of Life that controls the destiny of men. It operates through the minds of men, through the power of thought. The Philosophy of Individual Achievement set forth in Mental Dynamite was designed for the purpose of aiding men in the mastery and control of this great wheel, to the end that it may yield them an abundance of all they desire or need and bring enduring happiness. Remember, you who are beginning the study of this philosophy, that this same wheel which "prevents any man from being always fortunate," provides, also, that no man shall be "always unfortunate," if he will take possession of his mind and use it.

—Napoleon Hill

Contents

Chapter One

Definiteness of Purpose

Through the lessons of this book, you will be provided with usable knowledge that would cost you a huge fortune if you acquired it, as it was originally organized, from the minds of Andrew Carnegie and more than five hundred other distinguished leaders in American business and industry. Among the persons whose successful experience is published here are Henry Ford, Thomas A. Edison, Stuart Austin Wier, Cyrus H.K. Curtis, Edward Bok, Dr. Alexander Graham Bell, Dr. Elmer R. Gates, John Wanamaker, James J. Hill, Edwin C. Barnes, William Howard Taft, Charles M. Schwab, Theodore Roosevelt, Elbert H. Gary, Charles P. Steinmetz, and Woodrow Wilson.

For all practical purposes, you may assume that you are now entering a classroom in which your teachers will consist of more than five hundred of the men who have made America the "richest and freest", country known to civilization. Moreover, you will be privileged to acquire in this book the same knowledge that would have required over ten years of intense study had you procured it from its original source.

Through this book you will be schooled in an entire philosophy of success, complete and adequate in every respect for the needs of any person seeking the privilege of self-determination under the great American system of personal advancement. You will receive instruction that is not available at any price nor under any circumstances through any other source.

These lessons have been presented in a manner best suited to enable you to assimilate the knowledge they convey, with no effort on your part beyond a sincere desire to avail yourself of the secrets of achievement which are known to have been the foundation of almost all of the successful business leaders this country has produced.

In, thus departing from the usual academic style of presenting knowledge, the author has kept in mind the fact that this book is for men and women in all walks of life, whose educational background, occupation, and family responsibilities make it necessary for them to acquire practical knowledge by the shortest and quickest method available. The author has had in mind, too, the fact that this book is intended as a "family" schooling and should therefore be presented in an easy, readable style that will be interesting to young men and young women who have not yet finished high school or college as well as to the adult members of the family. Every principle of individual achievement here presented has been tested and tried in the great crucible of practical experience.

You can read these lessons in a few hours, but more than thirty years of careful research made it possible for you to do this. Moreover, this research was carried on by practical businessmen who acquired their experience by the trial and error method, over a long period of years.

Read slowly and digest that which you read, as you go along. The most important part is not in these lessons but in your mind. The major purpose of this chapter is not that of suggesting to you what your definite goal in life should be but rather to bring to your attention the necessity of your choosing a major objective as a starting point toward individual achievement.

Mark the paragraphs which impress you most as you read and come back to these for a more detailed analysis when time permits. It will be helpful if two or more people form a study club for the purpose of reading and analyzing the lessons together. The benefits of this plan will become more obvious after you finish the lesson on the Master Mind in the next chapter.

Somewhere in this book, you will find yourself—that "other self," which will throw off all the chains of limitation that previously bound you and reveal to you a veritable giant of power asleep in your brain, needing only some outside force to awaken it. You will find this awakening force. It will come in the form of an idea that you will pick up as you read and think.

To begin with, there are 17 major principles of success and every person who attains the objective of his major goal, in any undertaking, must use some combination of these principles. I shall name first, the most important. It stands at the head of the list of the 17 principles of achievement because no one has ever been known to succeed without applying it. You may call it the principle of Definiteness of Purpose. Study any person who is known to be a permanent success and you will find that he has a Definite Major Goal; he has a plan for the attainment of this goal; he devotes the major portion of his thoughts and his efforts to the attainment of this purpose.

Everyone wishes for the better things of life, such as money, a good position, fame, and recognition; but most people never go far beyond the "wishing" stage. Men who know exactly what they want of life and are determined to get it do not stop with wishing. They intensify their wishes into a Burning Desire, and back that desire with continuous effort based on a sound plan.

The first step from poverty to riches is the most difficult.

All riches and all material things that anyone acquires through self-effort begin in the form of a clear, concise mental picture of the thing one seeks. When that picture grows, or has been forced to the proportions of an obsession, it is taken over by the subconscious mind through some hidden law of nature. From that point on one is drawn, attracted, or guided in the direction of the physical equivalent of the mental picture. I shall come back to this subject of the subconscious mind many times before we finish, as it is one of the vital factors in connection with all outstanding achievements.

It has long been a mystery to some people why men with little or no schooling often succeed, while men with extensive schooling often fail. Look carefully and you will discover that great successes are the result of understanding and the use of a positive mental attitude through which nature aids men in converting their aims and purposes into their physical and financial equivalent. Mental attitude is the quality of mind which gives power to one's thoughts and plans.

The length of time which it takes for one's mental attitude to begin attracting the physical and financial requisites of one's major purpose depends entirely upon the nature and extent of one's desires and the control one exercises over his mind in keeping it free from fear and doubt and self-imposed limitations. This sort of control comes through constant vigilance, wherein one keeps his mind free of all negative thoughts and leaves it open for the influx and the guidance of Infinite Intelligence. Definiteness of purpose involving a hundred dollars, for example, might be translated into its financial equivalent in a few days, or even a few hours, or a few minutes, whereas, desire for a million dollars might call for considerably more time, depending to some extent on what one had to give in return for the million dollars.

The best way to describe the time necessary for the translation of a definite purpose into its physical or financial equivalent can be accurately stated by determining the exact time necessary to deliver the service, or the equivalent in value one intends to give in return for the object of that purpose.

Before I finish describing the most important principles of achievement, I hope to be able to prove to you that there is a definite connection between giving and getting. Generally speaking, riches and material things that men get are the effect of some form of useful service they have rendered.

The only known way of insuring that a definite purpose will be carried out to a full realization, through the forces of natural law working through the minds of men, is by first establishing a cause for such realization, through useful service, rendered in a spirit of harmony.

A well-disciplined mind is capable of holding and acting upon a definite major purpose without any form of outside, or artificial aid. The undisciplined mind needs a crutch to lean upon while dealing with a definite major purpose. The best method to be followed, by one with an undisciplined mind, is that of writing down a complete description of one's major purpose and then adopting the habit of reading it aloud at least once every day. The act of writing down one's major purposes forces one to be specific as to its nature. The act of habitual reading fixes the nature of the purpose in the mind, where it can be picked up by the subconscious mind and acted upon.

The good there is in money consists of the use to which it is put and not in the mere possession of it. Generally speaking, the man who earns his own money acquires, along with it some of the necessary wisdom as to its constructive use.

If you want a practical illustration of this reasoning, look at what happens to the boy or girl who is brought up by rich parents and is made to feel from early childhood that individual effort in the accumulation of riches is unnecessary. I have never known of a single instance in which a boy brought up in this fashion came within sight of the business acumen and achievements of his father. The real joy of having money comes from earning it; not from receiving it as a gift. •

We have more opportunities in America for the making of fortunes in return for useful service than in all other countries combined. This is a new country. Our resources have only been tapped. Every day brings on new endeavours to open hundreds of new roads of opportunity: Today it's the automobile and the aeroplane—industries in their infancy. Their development opens fields for thousands of young men with imagination, skill, and initiative.

Our only lack of opportunities is going to be a shortage of imagination, self-reliance and initiative which will be needed to man the future of this country. The whole world is turning to America for new ideas, new inventions, new opportunities for skill and imagination. Look around you everywhere and you will see that this is but the budding age of stupendous opportunity on every hand.

In the field of Life Insurance, there will be great opportunities for men and women to render useful service and make themselves financially independent. The institution of Life Insurance is rapidly becoming the major medium for the development of the habit of saving for millions of our people. The Life Insurance agent of the future will become a teacher as well as a salesman; he will teach people to budget their time and their expenditures by systematic investment in insurance. Keep your eyes on this field, because it represents one of the major pillars of our great American economic system. It will give profitable employment to hundreds of thousands of men and women whose services to the people will be no less useful than the services of the clergymen, or the school teachers. The selling of Life Insurance will become one of the most recognized professions that will pay as well as or better than most of the learned professions. The sale of Life Insurance will be reduced to a science, and eventually it will be taught in the colleges.

A man's achievements correspond with unerring certainty to the philosophy with which he relates himself to others. If you follow through your willingness to give something in return for the knowledge you desire, you are certain to make yourself so useful to the world that it will be compelled to reward you in terms of your own choice. This is the spirit of true Americanism.

Every person who seeks personal success in America should both understand and respect the fundamentals of Americanism. Those who neglect or refuse to give loyal support to the institutions of Americanism may unconsciously contribute to the downfall of these supporting pillars, thereby cutting the very foundation from under their own opportunities for personal achievement. It is obvious that no individual may enjoy permanent success if he is out of step with the forces which have given him his opportunity to succeed.

The Six Pillars of Americanism

You can best describe Americanism by analyzing the six major pillars which distinguish this country from all others, viz.:

1. Our American form of Government, as it was originally written into the Constitution of the United States, providing the fullest possible measure of right to individual liberty, freedom of thought, freedom of speech, freedom of worship, and above all, freedom of individual initiative that gives to every citizen the privilege of choosing his own occupation and setting his own price upon his knowledge, skill, and experience. No other country in the world offers its citizens such an abundant choice of opportunities for the marketing of his services as those provided under our form of government.
2. Our Industrial System, with its matchless natural resources of leadership and raw materials, coordinated, as it is, with our American Spirit of Democracy, and supported by our American form of government through which it is protected in every manner possible from the competition of other countries. So long as there is harmony and understanding and sympathetic cooperation between leaders of industry and the officials of our government, every citizen will benefit, directly or indirectly, by our expanding industrial system. If the time ever comes when the leaders of the government and the leaders of industry neglect or refuse to work in harmony toward a common end, the weight of their short-sightedness will fall heavily on the economic life of every citizen. This is definitely becoming an industrial nation. Industry not only supplies a major portion of the income for men who work for wages, but it absorbs a major portion of the products of

agriculture, and it is the major source of support for lawyers, doctors, dentists, engineers, educators, churches and others engaged in professional work. There is no way of separating "Americanism" from industry without destroying one of the strongest and most important of the six pillars.

3. Our banking system, providing, as it does, the life-blood which keeps our industrial system and our agriculture and our business and professional systems active and flexible at a cost that is not a burden to anyone. Understand the nature of the service being rendered by our banking system and you will be forever done with the ignorant few who cry out against the imaginary sins of "Wall Street." Every well-informed person knows that in this country we have a twin system of government, with a political division operating in Washington and a financial division operating in New York. When these two branches of our form of national life operate harmoniously, we have prosperous times. Moreover, we have the resources of both political and financial economy to compete successfully with any other country in the world. When these two branches of our national life become antagonistic, as they have done from time to time in the past, we are cursed with "panics" and other ills that damage every citizen. The banking houses are just as essential to the successful operation of our system of living as are the merchandising stores and business offices. As a matter of fact, no form of merchandising or business could be carried on successfully without access to a ready supply of cash or credit, which the banks supply.
4. Our Life Insurance System, serving, as it does, as the people's greatest national institution of individual savings, and providing our economic system with a form of flexibility that would not be available through the banking system alone. No other American institution provides the people with a source of savings that gives the individual protection for his family and at the same time releases his mind from worry in connection with the possibility of approaching old age and its economic uncertainties. The institution of Life Insurance, which is definitely a part of the fundamentals of

America, provides a system which makes it unnecessary for any physically sound person to humiliate himself in old age by the acceptance of charity.

5. Our National Spirit of Love for Liberty and our demand for the privilege of self-determination, as expressed by the pioneers in industry and government, and the national love of freedom of speech, thought and action, which were the distinguishing characteristics of the great leaders produced by America in the past.
6. Our National Sense of Justice, which inspires us to fight for the protection of the weak as well as the strong, and has never tolerated territorial annexation by conquest without adequate compensation.

Under these six headings, you will find everything of major importance that distinguishes this country from all others. *Anything which weakens any of the six pillars of Americanism, undermines correspondingly the whole of our national life*. It is not enough for an individual to refrain from doing or saying anything that would weaken these pillars; but it is the duty of every loyal American to defend these fundamentals against all who endeavour to weaken or destroy any portion of them.

We Americans should think and talk less of our rights, and more of our duties and privileges as individuals in protecting the very foundation on which our rights and privileges are founded. It is plainly the duty of every citizen to make the defense of these fundamental pillars of Americanism a definite part of his *Major Purpose in Life*.

There is a growing tendency in this country for men with a radical trend of mind to find fault with our form of government, our industrial system, our banking system, and about everything else that represents the basic pillars of our Americanism. Careful analysis of these men will disclose the truth that they are suffering with some form of inferiority complex which expresses itself in a desire to discredit all who succeed and who are accepted as leaders in business and industry.

Some of these radicals are men of great brilliancy of mind on most subjects except that of economic and social philosophy. Some are foreign born, some are American born. You will find them in politics, in some of the churches, in many public schools and colleges, in the labour unions, and in nearly every other calling. Their efforts to destroy our nation, whether based on sincere ignorance or out and out sinister motives, should be met blow for blow. They should not be permitted to destroy the world's greatest nation merely because we preach and practice the right of free speech in this country. The right of free speech does not carry with it a license to libel respectable men merely because they have been successful! Since the beginning of civilization, wealth has found its way into the hands of men who think accurately; men with definiteness of purpose; men with keenness of imagination and the initiative to translate imagination into useful service. No amount of preachment by radicals can change this, and it is this very truth that has led me to the belief that the very best method of distributing wealth is that of distributing the principles of achievement by which wealth is procured.

In speaking of the great resources of this country, it should be always kept in mind that the greatest of these is not the money in the banks, nor the minerals in the ground, nor the trees in the forest, nor the richness of our soil; but it is the mental attitude, and the imagination, and the pioneering spirit of the men who have mixed experience and education with these raw materials, thereby transforming them into various types of useful service for our own people and for the people of other nations.

The real wealth of this nation is not any material, tangible thing. Our real wealth consists of the intangible power of thought, as it is expressed by our leaders who understand and apply the philosophy of individual achievement. It reflects itself in broader visions, wider horizons, greater ambitions, and initiative. Anyone who misses this truth will fail to understand why ours is the "richest and freest" country in the world.

The principle of *Definiteness of Purpose* obviously is a necessity to all who succeed, since no one may achieve success without first knowing precisely what he wants. It is interesting to know that approximately 98 out of 100 people are totally without a major goal, and it is significant that approximately the same percentage of people are regarded as failures.

The principle of definiteness of purpose, to be of enduring value, must be adopted and applied as a daily habit. Absence of this habit leads to another habit that is fatal to success, and that is the habit of drifting. We have found that salesmen sell more merchandise when they are given definite sales quotas than when they sell without quotas.

A good definition of success is "The power with which to acquire whatever one demands of life, without violating the rights of others." No person without definiteness of purpose can wield enough power to be sure of getting anything except that which no one else desires. You will observe that men with power are men who reach decisions quickly and change them slowly, if they change them at all. Decision is a twin brother of definiteness. These are two words with which to conjure—Definiteness and Decision. They represent a positive mental attitude without which no worthwhile success can be achieved in any calling. These qualities are an important part of the mental attitude of all great leaders.

If you will analyze my definition of success, you will see that there is no element of luck about it. A man may and sometimes men do, fall into opportunities through mere chance, or luck, but they have a queer way of falling out of these opportunities the first time opposition overtakes them. You will find this theory substantiated by studying those who inherit money which they did not earn and those who are lifted into high positions through what is commonly called "pull." A man may come into possession of opportunity by inheritance or pull, but he can stay in possession of it only by push, and that calls for Definiteness of Purpose. The person who tries to go through life on "pull" and luck finds Old Man Fate standing just around the comer with a stuffed club, and it is not stuffed with cotton. When the blow falls on his head, he can't take it.

Personal power is acquired through a combination of individual traits and habits. Briefly, the ten qualities of personal power (which I call the ten-point rule of personal power) are these:

(a) The habit of definiteness of purpose
(b) Promptness of decision
(c) Soundness of character (intentional honesty)
(d) Strict discipline over one's emotions
(e) Obsessional desire to render useful service
(f) Thorough knowledge of one's occupation
(g) Tolerance on all subjects
(h) Loyalty to one's personal associates and faith in a Supreme Being

(i) Enduring thirst for knowledge

(j) Alertness of imagination

You will observe that this ten-point rule embraces only the traits which anyone may develop. You will observe, also, that these traits lead to the development of a form of personal power which can be used without "violating the rights of others." That is the only form of personal power anyone can afford to wield.

The old adage, "knowledge is power," is not quite true. Knowledge never is power until it has been expressed in some term of useful service. The space a man occupies in life corresponds, in minute exactness, to the quality and the quantity of service he renders, plus the mental attitude in which he renders the service. Men who wield great personal power, if they remain powerful, must understand and apply the Q+Q+C formula. That is, the quality of their service must be right, the quantity must be right, and their conduct must be agreeable. You might state this truth in another way, viz.: Quality of service, plus quantity of service, plus mode of conduct, equals the degree of success one will command.

Again observe that the QQC formula represents only qualities which anyone may develop. The formula has nothing whatever to do with luck, unless it may be said that those who apply this formula seem to have luck on their side in a great majority of their experiences. The fellow who is always complaining about not getting the "breaks," or that luck is against him, is merely using this excuse as an alibi with which to apologize for laziness, indifference, or lack of ambition. The fellow who wants something for nothing will be quick enough to complain of "bad luck" when failure overtakes him. The successful man says little or nothing about luck, because he has a more dependable philosophy on which to lean. He makes or largely influences his own "breaks."

John Wanamaker served the people through one of the greatest retail stores in America. When asked, he replied quickly enough, that his success as a merchant was due entirely to definite principles of achievement, and not to luck.

James J. Hill built the Great Northern Railroad System with definiteness of purpose, and he made of it a huge success. His rise from the lowly position of telegraph operator to the position of directing head of a great railroad system was systematically planned. At no time did he rely upon luck for the acquisition of personal power.

Thomas A. Edison gave the world the incandescent electric light bulb, the talking machine, the moving picture, and a score or more of other aids to mankind; but no part of his success was achieved through luck. The very fact that Edison met with more than ten thousand failures before he found a method by which to harness electricity and make it serve to light a lamp, proves that he had no faith in luck. Measure these men, and all others of their type, by the ten-point rule (already described) for the development of personal power, and you will be forced to the conclusion that they succeeded because they developed and used these ten qualities. Success is the result of mind power properly organized, controlled, and directed with definiteness of purpose.

Let me caution you, however, against jumping to the conclusion that Definiteness of Purpose, by itself, is sufficient for the achievement of success. There are sixteen other major principles of individual achievement, with some or all of which definiteness of purpose must be combined. The choice of a definite major purpose is but the starting point toward success. The personal power with which to translate definiteness of purpose into its physical or financial equivalent comes through understanding and use of other principles of achievement.

Another important characteristic connected with personal power is the necessity of understanding the difference between power that is acquired with the full consent and approval of all who are affected by it and power that is forced upon others without their consent. Lack of understanding of this difference has brought failure to many who would, otherwise, have been great successes. Study the ten-point rule carefully and you will be convinced that it leads only to that form of power which is acquired with the consent and the cooperation of other people.

In the city of Detroit, there is a man by the name of Henry Ford whose philosophy of human relationship promises to lift him into a dominating position in the industrial world. I want you to go to Detroit and meet Mr. Ford, for the time is coming when he is sure to dominate the automobile industry. Study this man carefully, weigh his philosophy accurately, and observe how definitely he is acquiring personal power by applying the ten-point rule. Definiteness of Purpose is his obsession. He knows enough to put all his eggs in one basket and then guard that basket carefully, through definiteness of purpose.

Simply stated, his purpose has been that of making a low priced, dependable automobile. His was a "one track" mind, but it led him precisely where he wished to go. His philosophy has brought him great wealth and a nation of friends and patrons. It will, perhaps, enable him to occupy more space in the world than any other industrialist of his time.

Look what F.W. Woolworth accomplished through his understanding of the ten-point rule for the development of personal power. His philosophy was the same as that of Henry Ford. He built one of the tallest buildings in America; built it on nickels and dimes that other people had spent carelessly. He, too, had a "one-track" mind. He took one simple, unique idea of merchandising and made it yield him a huge fortune. The strangest thing about his success is the simplicity of his business policy. He had no patent rights on his merchandising plan, yet he has but few imitators, and it is for that reason that he moves with definiteness of purpose while most of the other merchants lack such a purpose. They have a different policy for every item of merchandise they sell. Woolworth has but one policy for the sale of all his merchandise. Study this man, and all others whose efforts are based on definiteness of purpose, and you will be forever cured of the notion that success and luck have anything in common.

These ten qualities of personal power must become habits. Occasional application of the qualities will be of little value. The man who only applies them when they serve his immediate purpose, but ignores them when they appear to be unprofitable, will never have enduring power. The qualities of personal power must become so definitely a part of a man's character that they take on a spiritual nature. This cannot be accomplished in a day, or a week, or perhaps in a year. It will be helpful if an individual writes out a list of these ten qualities and carefully grades himself on each of them once every day. By this procedure they will be taken over by the subconscious mind and made a part of his character. But one must not stop by merely rating himself daily; he must put these qualities into practice in all his relationships with others. An ounce of practice is worth a million tons of theory.

After the individual blends the ten qualities into his own character through habit, he must make it his business to endeavour by every practical means at his command to induce his associates to appropriate and use them; especially his more intimate associates, such as the members of his family, his personal friends, and those with whom he works. It has been said that "The best way to acquire the virtues of sound character is by helping others, through example, to acquire them."

Successful men of the past, generally speaking, acquired their knowledge of the principles of successful achievement by the trial and error system. But that is a long and costly method. That is why so many men have failed, although their aims and purposes were worthy enough. Good intentions and high resolves are not sufficient for the achievement of permanent success. One must know the rules by which personal power may be acquired, a form of knowledge that is available only to those who understand and apply all the principles of achievement.

We are here concerned only with that form of success which is achieved through deliberate planning and which remains permanently. The man who achieves success through the application of the success principles may, through some mistake of judgment, or for some cause over which he has no control, temporarily lose the fruits of his success; but he will know how to recoup his losses. He will understand how to build a new success out of an old defeat. Moreover, the man who is master of the principles of success quickly learns how to convert stumbling blocks into stepping stones; he learns how to extract useful knowledge from temporary defeat, and above all, he learns the difference between temporary defeat and failure. If he meets with temporary defeat, he stages a quick comeback and profits by the experience. He supplants the spirit of defeatism with the spirit of faith. He knows how to remove the self-imposed limitations that hold most men back, because he realizes that most limitations are nothing but states of mind.

To the master of the principles of achievement, the experience of temporary defeat is nothing but a signal to rebuild his plans and increase his determination to win. In brief, these principles provide one with a philosophy that recognizes no such circumstance as failure. Accurate understanding of the philosophy of achievement makes one success-conscious; it converts one's mind into a powerful magnet that attracts to him an exact equivalent of his own mental attitude, as it is reflected in his plans, aims, and purposes.

The master of this philosophy finds an abundance of opportunity placed in his path as if by some queer stroke of magic. He finds people going out of their way to lend him cooperation, and this without any apparent efforts or requests on his part. You might say that the individual first masters the philosophy of achievement; then it masters everything that gets in his way; and all this happens through some strange mixture of mind chemistry which science does not understand, nor does science undertake to explain the source of its power.

It is not likely that anyone who understands the principles of achievement will ever become a "quitter" because all who understand the philosophy know that it provides sufficient power to meet any ordinary human emergency! It will put sounder legs under a man's religion, no matter what may be his religious beliefs. It will give the salesman more ability, regardless of the commodity he is selling. It will make of one a more loyal American because the philosophy is literally the very foundation on which this nation was developed. Mastery of the principles will bring one riches in terms of enduring friendships, peace of mind, harmony in family relationships, financial security, and that state of mind known as happiness. The philosophy is complete in that it helps all who master it to negotiate their way through life with a minimum amount of friction, resistance, and opposition from their fellow men. Once you get this conception you, will know that it brings one very close to an understanding of Infinite Intelligence through which the individual recognizes his proper relationship to himself, to all others, and to his Maker.

Any dominating idea, plan, thought, or purpose that is held in the mind through a strong desire for its realization, is picked up by the subconscious mind and translated into its physical or financial equivalent by whatever practical means are available. Let us here stress the fact that any desire, plan, or purpose which is backed by faith in its fulfillment and emotionalized by a strong desire for its fulfillment takes precedence in the magical operations of the subconscious mind and is acted upon more quickly than any plan or purpose placed in the mind with nothing but cold reason as its motivating force. This applies with equal certainty to both negative and positive states of mind. A mind that is dominated by thoughts which dwell continuously upon fear and poverty will lead to misery and failure, just as definitely as thoughts which dwell upon faith and opulence will lead to success.

It is highly important that you understand the truth that your "mental attitude" is a two-way entrance into your mind, the mental attitude of faith leading into a reservoir of power that automatically translates your desires, plans, and purposes into their exact physical equivalent, and the mental attitudes of fear and doubt leading into an equally definite reservoir of power which converts your desires, plans, and purposes into certain nothingness.

With definite knowledge of what I am saying I can tell you that this is the way the mind works. Neither me nor any other person has ever been able to tell how or why the mind works in this manner. It is no mere phrase of speech, nor is it any exaggeration to say that "Whatever man can believe, man can do." It is a well-known fact that man's only limitations are those which he sets up in his own mind. If this were not true, how could we account for the achievements of a man like Thomas A. Edison, who, with but three months of schooling, controlled and made such practical use of the powers of his mind that he became the world's most distinguished inventor?

If this were not true, how shall we account for the achievements of Henry Ford, who, starting at scratch, with but little of that form of education known as a common-school education, belted the earth with the physical products of his mind and accumulated a huge fortune in return for his service?

Careful analysis of the achievements of such men as Ford and Edison is sufficient to convince any thinking person that men who move with Definiteness of Purpose, backed by faith in their ability to achieve the object of their purpose, project the powers of their minds into the very reservoir of Infinite Intelligence, wherein may be found the answer to all human problems, the fulfillment of all human desires.

It is not the purpose of this book to undertake to lead the reader into an intricate or abstract study of all the working principles of the mind, or to present an intricate and abstract discourse in psychology, but it is the purpose to show by convincing evidence that in a country such as ours, with its superabundance of everything people need or desire, there is no legitimate reason for anyone remaining in want. Acquisition of the material things we need and desire begins, always, in a clear concept of what we want, plus a burning desire for its attainment. In a country such as ours, the only thing in which the people are lacking is sufficient faith to take possession of their own minds and to make the fullest use of those minds. It has been proved too many times for its soundness to be doubted, that "mental attitude," and not mere knowledge or education, is the real source of all achievements.

I have said that the subconscious mind accepts and carries out the dominating thoughts of the mind which have been mixed with emotion, whether the emotion be positive or negative; that it translates thoughts of limitation, fear, and doubt into certain failure, just as surely as it translates thoughts of faith into success. Let us take inventory of some well-known experiences which prove the soundness of this statement.

Take, for example, the experiences of 1929, the beginning of the most extended and devastating depression this country has ever known. When millions of people throughout the country started to gamble in the stock market, and their frenzied trading caused a crash in the market through which they lost their money, their highly emotionalized minds began to broadcast vibrations of fear, and those vibrations extended themselves in every direction until they reached the minds of other millions of people who were not gambling, resulting, finally, in a state of mass fear that paralyzed all banking, caused runs on banks, tied up the machinery of industry, and closed down normal business activities on a scale without precedent.

Here we were, jumping, almost overnight, from opulence and plenty into panic and poverty, despite the fact that there was exactly the same amount of all forms of riches in this country during the panic as before it started. The affairs of the people of the world change with their change of "mental attitude" as definitely and as regularly as the rise and flow of the tides of the oceans. Out of this truth came that old saying that "Success attracts success and failure attracts failure."

Accurate analysis of more than 25,000 men and women who were classified as "failures" established positive evidence of the working principles of the mind through which these unfortunate people brought about their own misfortunes. Listed without any attempt to classify these causes of failure as to their relative effects, these are some of the major causes:

(a) The widespread habit of accepting the limitation of poverty, as reflected by a willingness to be contented with the three bare necessities of life: food, shelter, and clothing. I am not here going into the causes of lack of ambition which result in people not aiming above a desire for more than the necessities of life; I am merely analyzing a well-known fact to show that in spite of the vast riches of our great country a majority of the people have no definite purpose beyond the procuring of a mere living.

(b) Failure to recognize that which every psychologist knows: that neither external matters nor circumstances have any influence over the "mental attitude" of anyone, save only those who, through refusal to take possession of their own minds and use them, impose limitations upon their minds. It has been proved, times too numerous to mention, that any normal mind can break these poverty limitations any time the individual takes possession of his mind and becomes determined to use it for the acquisition of riches. Andrew Carnegie proved that his mind had the power to remove self-limitations when he became determined to quit the work of common labour and begin the more profitable work of organizing and operating a great steel industry. Thomas A. Edison made a similar demonstration of the powers of his mind when he became determined to leave his lowly work as a tramp telegraph operator and become the world's greatest inventor. Strange as it may seem, the very mindpower with which he made the switch from the life of a tramp to that of a highly successful inventor, became the power with which he penetrated the secrets of Infinite Intelligence and uncovered Nature's secrets.

(c) Failure to recognize the important difference between wishing for a thing and being determined to get it. Everyone wishes for the better things of life, and many make the fatal mistake of believing that a wish is the same as a clearly defined definite purpose, backed by a burning desire for its possession. The difference is precisely the difference between success and failure.

(d) The habit of allowing the mind to become limited through some form of fear, and an accepted inferiority. Many people who are born in an environment of poverty, and those who are temporarily cast into association with those who have accepted poverty as their lot, set up in their own minds insurmountable barriers by such a phobia. Every year millions of children are born in poverty and never learn that they can make themselves financially independent. From early childhood until death they use their mind-power in reverse gear, condemning themselves to poverty as surely as if their prayers were for misfortune.

(e) Failure to develop the habit of initiative, a failure which usually may be traced to its prototype, the belief in the individual's inferiority. Very obviously those who suffer with lack of initiative never will take possession of their own minds or anything else.

(f) Shortness of vision, the habit of setting up, voluntarily or by neglect, limitations upon the use of their mind-power by not aiming for any station in life above mediocrity. Man's achievements end where his limitations of mind-power begin, no matter what may be the cause of the limitations. Those who seek little usually attain just what they seek.

(g) Lack of attention to the importance of the development of an attractive personality by learning traits, habits, and skills which unselfishly serve others. The failure to forget self. Those who love themselves will have few rivals.

(h) Development of the habit of procrastination, which leads to the habit of perpetual drifting through life and taking the line of least resistance at every turn. Lethargy and political expediency never built an empire.

(i) Choosing as their closest associates people who suffer with a well-defined poverty-consciousness and others of limited vision. Mental attitudes are contagious. That is why men who are known as successes make it a part of their personal responsibility to associate with men of ambition, who refuse to accept the limitations of life.

(j) Lack of faith and an inadequate understanding of the principle of prayer, through which the subconscious mind transfers to Infinite Intelligence a definite picture of one's mental attitude.

Here you have a brief but accurate description of the major sources through which men condemn themselves to misery, poverty and failure. As a starting point toward success, take inventory of yourself by determining how many of these causes of failure you are sheltering in your own mind.

Ideas are the only assets which have no fixed value. They are the beginning of all achievements; they form the foundation of all fortunes; they are the starting point of all inventions; ideas have mastered the air above us, and they have enabled us to harness and use the energy known as ether, through which any brain may communicate with any other brain.

Ideas begin as the result of Definiteness of Purpose. The talking machine was nothing but an abstract idea until Edison submitted it to the subconscious portion of his brain where it was projected into the great reservoir of Infinite Intelligence and flashed back to his mind in the form of a definite plan for its mechanical perfection.

The Anti-Saloon League was nothing but a rather vague sort of an idea that existed nowhere except in the minds of the two people who gave birth to it, in the village of Westerville, Ohio, over forty years ago; but there came a time when that idea, backed by Definiteness of Purpose, wiped out the saloons. I am not here trying to present the merits of the idea. I am only calling attention to the power of ideas when they are persistently backed by the human mind.

Al Capone gave birth to an idea, as the direct result of the changed social conditions brought about by the work of the Anti- Saloon League, and despite the unsavory nature of his idea, he placed Definiteness of Purpose back of it and thereby gave it such momentum that the entire forces of the law enforcement agencies of the powerful United States Government were required to stop the damage his idea was doing. Thus, it will be recognized that ideas, backed by Definiteness of Purpose, work just as definitely for harm as for good, but above all they work.

The Rotary Club movement began as an idea, originally created in the mind of a lawyer for the purpose of extending his personal acquaintanceship and thereby building up his law practice without violating the ethics of the legal profession. The Rotary Club idea was humble enough at the start; but it was backed by Definiteness of Purpose until it now belts the entire earth and serves as a medium by which men come together in a spirit of friendly fellowship in nearly every country of the world.

The New World was discovered and brought under the influence of civilization as the result of an idea backed by Definiteness of Purpose expressed in the single mind of a humble sailor. The time may come, soon, when this newly discovered world may become the last frontier of civilization, thereby lifting the idea back of its discovery to first position in the important things which affect mankind.

Christianity, the greatest single power for good known to the world, began as an idea in the mind of one humble carpenter. Through persistent application of the Principle of Definiteness of Purpose this idea has gone marching onward for nearly two thousand years, and it may well be expected to save the present trend toward destruction of civilization, if men will practice its tenets.

That which men believe, talk about, and expect has a queer way of making its appearance in one form or another. Let those of us who are struggling to free ourselves from the limitations of poverty and misery not forget this great truth, as it applies to an individual as well as to a nation of people.

Let us now turn our attention to the working principle through which thoughts, ideas, plans, and purposes placed in the conscious mind find their way into the subconscious section of the brain, where they are picked up and carried out to their logical conclusion by Infinite Intelligence.

Transfer of thought from the conscious to the subconscious mind may be hastened by the simple process of stepping up or stimulating the vibrations of thought through faith, fear, or any other intensified emotion, such as enthusiasm, a burning desire based on Definiteness of Purpose, or hatred and jealousy. Thoughts based upon faith appear to have precedence over all others in the matter of definiteness and speed with which they are handed over to the subconscious mind. The speed with which the power of faith works has given rise to the belief that certain phenomena are the result of "miracles." Psychologists recognize no such phenomenon as a miracle today, claiming that everything that is and everything that happens is the result of a definite cause. Be this as it may, it is a well-known fact that the person who is capable of freeing his mind of all self-imposed limitations, through the mental attitude known as faith, generally finds the solution to all his problems, regardless of their nature.

Infinite Intelligence, while it is not an automatic solver of riddles, carries out to a logical conclusion any clearly defined idea, aim, purpose, or desire that is submitted to the subconscious mind in a mental attitude of perfect faith. However, Infinite Intelligence never attempts to modify, change or otherwise alter any thought that is submitted to it, and it has never been known to act upon a mere wish or indefinite idea, thought or purpose. Get this truth well-grounded in your mind, and you will find yourself in possession of sufficient power to solve your daily problems with much less effort than most people put into worrying over their problems.

So-called "hunches" often are signals indicating that Infinite Intelligence is trying to reach and influence the conscious mind. They usually come in response to some idea, plan, purpose, or desire, or some fear that has been handed over to Infinite Intelligence through the subconscious mind. Hunches should be treated civilly and examined carefully since they often convey, either in whole or in part, information of the greatest value to an individual. These hunches often make their appearance many hours, days, or weeks after the thought that inspires them has reached the reservoir of Infinite Intelligence; meanwhile, the individual often has forgotten the original thought that inspired them.

This is a deep, profound subject about which even the wisest of people know but little. It becomes a self-revealing subject only upon deep meditation. Many believe that it is in the manner described that the power of prayer operates. Many believe, also, that Definiteness of Purpose, backed by faith, is of itself the finest of prayers. Understand the principle of the mind here described and you will have a dependable clue as to why prayer sometimes brings that which one desires, while at times it brings that which one does not wish. Consider the fact that most people turn to prayer only after everything else has failed them, generally in the hour of emergency when their minds are saturated with fear and doubt, and you may have the answer as to why prayer often brings that which one least desires. If you go to prayer with your mind wholly or partly filled with fear or doubt, Infinite Intelligence seems to accommodate by carrying out to its logical conclusion the precise mental attitude in which you pray.

The sort of faith that brings results, without exception, is that mental attitude in which one sees the object of one's desires already in hand, even before going to prayer. This sort of mental attitude comes only through preparation and discipline of the mind. Sometimes the discipline may be the result of deliberate effort on the part of an individual; at other times it may be the result of some great sorrow or deeply-seated disappointment that forces one to turn to the "inner self" for consolation, wherein consists the truth that failure sometimes is a blessing in disguise.

A careful analysis of civilization will impress you with the profound way in which the human race is chastised every so often, through some great calamity such as a world depression, thus giving logic to the theory that failure and disappointment are weapons of discipline with which human beings are forced to turn to their spiritual natures for aid. The ten-year depression which spread over the entire world from 1929 to 1939 might easily be conceived to have been Nature's own way of forcing the people of the world to reclaim the spiritual values they so prodigiously wasted during the First World War.

No great leader has ever been known to achieve noteworthy success without drawing upon spiritual forces. There is a power greater than man himself, and it is often incomprehensible to the finite mind of man. An acceptance of this truth is essential to the successful culmination of any definite purpose. The great philosophers of all ages, from Plato and Socrates on down to Emerson and the moderns, and the great Statesmen of our times, from George Washington down to Abraham Lincoln, have been known to have turned to the inner self in times of emergency. No great and enduring success has ever been achieved, and none will ever be achieved, except by those who recognize and use the spiritual powers of the infinite as sensed in their inner selves. Failure to recognize this profound truth may be the major reason why the world is now so nearly bankrupt spiritually! No matter who you are, or what may be your calling, you will never come into possession of great power if you neglect or refuse to recognize and make use of your spiritual forces.

There was a man who was said to be the greatest Life Insurance salesman in America. For fifteen consecutive years he has been a member of the Million Dollar a Year Club, an organization of Life Insurance salesmen who sell a minimum of one million dollars of insurance annually. As "cool-headed and calculating" as he is said to be in connection with his business affairs, he never makes a call on a prospective purchaser of insurance without preparing his mind by at least an hour of introspective communion with his "inner self" during which he does away with his "coolheadedness" and substitutes in its place all the spiritual force he can command. It is another way of saying that he communed with God in prayer. He has discovered that Infinite Intelligence acts on his desire to serve his fellow men through the medium of Life Insurance, just as quickly and definitely as it acts on any other purpose.

This man makes no dramatic outward gestures in connection with his sales methods, nor does he feature his religious beliefs. His method of drawing upon the spiritual forces of his being for aid in his daily profession is something between himself and his Maker. It becomes manifest in a sincere desire to serve his fellow men. Somehow we cannot escape the belief that perhaps the quiet, unpretentious way in which this man goes about seeking the source of spiritual power within himself brings him much nearer to the source of all power than the methods of some men who advertise their religion in more dramatic ways. People who judged the late Thomas A. Edison, without knowing very much, if anything, about his personal beliefs, made the mistake of assuming that he became the world's most distinguished inventor because of his great reasoning power. The exact opposite to this belief is the real truth. The author was in the close confidence of Mr. Edison, over a long period of years, and he is in a position, therefore, to say that Mr. Edison's success was largely due to his habit of turning to the "inner man" for the solution of his most baffling problems. Mr. Edison understood, and used to the fullest, his spiritual estate. He was much more profoundly spiritual in nature than many people who proclaim deep-seated spiritual beliefs.

To many people it may also be something of a surprise to learn that Henry Ford's stupendous industrial and financial wisdom has its seat in his habit of drawing upon and using his spiritual forces. Mr. Ford never features, or advertises his spiritual belief, but be assured he knows that he owes his riches and his great achievements to his knowledge and use of the spiritual. Unlike the Dictators of Europe, who blatantly cry from the housetops that they are bound to win because God is on their side of the battle, Mr. Ford goes quietly about his business, and silently submits his every aim and purpose to the spiritual reservoirs of his soul. If one may judge him by his achievements, his system has the advantage of carrying him continuously forward, despite the opposition of powerful groups of men who, times without number, have tried to defeat him.

Andrew Carnegie once said, "Look out for the fellow who strengthens his aims and purposes with spiritual forces, for he is apt to challenge you at the post and pass you at the grand stand." When Mr. Carnegie looked into the future more than thirty years ago, and prophesied that Henry Ford would become the dominating factor in the automobile industry, he based his prophecy upon his knowledge of Mr. Ford's recognition and use of his spiritual estate.

A little while ago the publisher of *Think and Grow Rich* (a one-volume interpretation of a portion of the philosophy of individual achievement) began to receive telegraphic orders for that book from the stores in and near Des Moines, Iowa. The orders called for immediate shipments of the book, by express. Neither the author of this volume nor the publisher knew what had caused this sudden stimulation of sales of the book in the vicinity of Des Moines until several weeks afterward, when the author received a letter from Mr. Edward P. Chase, of Des Moines, a Life Insurance salesman representing the Sun Life Assurance Company, in which he said:

"I am writing to express my grateful appreciation of your book, Think and Grow Rich. I followed its advice to the letter. As a result I received an idea which resulted in the sale of a two million dollar policy. The above is the largest single sale of its kind ever to be made in Des Moines."

The key sentence in Mr. Chase's letter is the second sentence: "I followed its advice to the letter." I wish to tell you briefly why Mr. Chase so easily converted the contents of a book into a sale of life insurance greater in amount than the average insurance agent sells in four years of hard effort. First of all, the book, which inspired this large business transaction, literally abounds in spiritual stimuli, a fact to which many of its quarter of a million readers could testify.

In one sentence Mr. Chase testifies that he read the book with an open mind and "followed its advice to the letter." When he went out to sell a two million dollar insurance policy, he took with him a Definiteness of Purpose that was supported by the irresistible power of faith. He didn't merely read the book, as some perhaps have done. He did not lay it aside in an attitude of cynicism with the thought that the principles it described might work, and then again they might not. He read it with an open mind, recognized the stimulating spiritual forces it described, appropriated those forces, and immediately put them to work in his business of selling life insurance.

Somewhere in the reading of the book Mr. Chase's mind established contact with the mind of the author, and that contact quickened his own mind so definitely and intensely that an idea was born. The idea was to sell a large insurance policy, perhaps the largest he had ever sold. The sale of that policy became his immediate definite major purpose. He moved on that purpose without delay and, behold! the objective was reached. No more time or effort was required to sell the two million dollar policy than might have been needed to sell a thousand dollar policy. As Mr. Carnegie so well stated, the man who is motivated by the spiritual "may challenge at the post and pass you at the grand stand," whether he is selling life insurance or digging ditches. There is simply no such reality as failure for the man who becomes acquainted with spiritual power and has faith in this power to use it as a means of mastering his problems.

As Mr. Carnegie once said, "A great weakness in some men is that they know too much! They know too many things which will not work." What he meant was this: Some people are so unfamiliar with the power of spiritual force that they neglect to use the power, depending on what they believe to be their own reasoning wisdom to get them through life. The truly great men are always open-minded and humble. The arrogant egotist never comes within arm's reach of Infinite Intelligence, without the aid of which man's accomplishments are small.

The mere casual reading of this book will not give its students the fullest benefits of the knowledge it conveys. There is more to the book than that which appears in its printed pages. There is "that something" hidden back of the lines of the printed page which can be uncovered only by the reader who reads with an open mind with a Definite Purpose, and with a determination to tune in and catch the spirit of the great steel master and the other distinguished men whose philosophy of achievement will be found throughout these lessons.

Vision is an asset of priceless value. But passive vision leads only to impractical day-dreaming. Mr. Carnegie described the principle of Definiteness of Purpose in plain English that any school boy or school girl can understand, but Definiteness of Purpose means nothing more than passive vision until and unless it is given life and action through the application of one's spiritual powers. Definiteness of Purpose is but the starting point toward success.

One's purpose must be lifted out of the passive category and clothed with the spiritual forces of action! One's major purpose, to ensure its realization to the fullest, must be given obsessional proportion. There is a definite formula through which this desirable end can be attained, and I come, now, to the presentation of this formula, viz.:

The formula for translation of definiteness of purpose into its physical equivalent

(a) Write out a full, clear statement of your Definite Major Purpose in life, sign it, commit it to memory and repeat it orally at least once daily. As you do this you should proceed as if your major purpose were a prayer, and your faith in your ability to acquire the object of your major purpose should be so definite that you can see yourself already in possession of it.

(b) On another page write out a clear statement of the plan or the plans by which you hope to attain the objective of your major purpose. It is important that you leave all plans sufficiently flexible so that you can alter, modify, change, or supplant them with better plans at any time you may feel the "inner urge" to do so. Remember, the object of repeating your major purpose daily is to impress it upon your subconscious mind after which it will be picked up and acted upon by Infinite Intelligence. Remember, too, that Infinite Intelligence may find its own plans for the translation of your purpose into its physical equivalent. Be always on the alert, therefore, for the signal to change your plans. The signal will come in the form of a sudden idea or "hunch" that will present itself to your mind, perhaps at a moment when you are least expecting it. When the call comes, do not hesitate but respond immediately and make whatever change of plans it inspires.

(c) When you write out a statement of your major purpose, include in your statement a definite time limit within which you desire its fulfillment. With the laws of nature, as with the laws of man, time is of vital importance. Legal contracts, to be enforceable, must have a reasonable time limit within which the terms of the contract must be carried out. The same is true in connection with a compact with Infinite

Intelligence. If no time limit is mentioned in connection with the acquisition of the object of one's major purpose, Infinite Intelligence may establish its own time. Infinite Intelligence has an abundance of time and, unless you establish your own time within which to achieve the object of your major purpose, Infinite Intelligence may not get around to its fulfillment in time to do you any good.

(d) Control your "mental attitude" during the period when you are repeating orally the written statement of your major purpose. Never begin this profound ceremony until you are completely alone, and do not begin it until you clear your mind of fear, doubt and worry. Infinite Intelligence acts upon and carries out the "mental attitude" in which you present your desires and demands. If you catch the full significance of this instruction, and form the habit of carrying it out faithfully, you will soon find yourself in possession of the key which will open the door to the reservoir of your spiritual estate at will.

What the written statement of your definite major purpose should contain

In order that no reader may be confused as to what subjects one's Definite Major Purpose should cover, the author presents the following skeleton outline as a guide:

(a) The first paragraph should state precisely the achievement one desires within the time limit chosen for the realization of one's major purpose.

(b) The second paragraph should describe clearly and definitely the exact quality and quantity of service one intends to give in return for the reward demanded. Let there be no illusions on this point. Infinite Intelligence never rewards people with something for nothing, nor does Infinite Intelligence favour the person who expects or demands pay out of proportion to the value of that which is given in return. Men can, and sometimes they do, cheat one another; *but no one has ever been known to cheat Infinite Intelligence*.

(c) The third paragraph should describe the "mental attitude" in which you intend to deliver the service you are to give in return for the money you demand. Your description should clearly state that you will relate yourself in a spirit of harmony toward every person who is in any manner affected by the service you render. Remember, as you carry out this instruction, that the people to whom you render service are affected by your "mental attitude" and your mode of personal conduct; that they respond in kind to your "frame of mind" the same as Infinite Intelligence takes notice of it. Here again, do not lose the profound significance of this instruction. If you do, your mistake may cost you the full results of your efforts.

(d) In the fourth paragraph, write out a clear description of the part you intend to take in fulfilling your duty as an American citizen, remembering, as you write, that no one has a right to enjoy the far-flung privileges of Americanism without definitely contributing something of value to perpetuate and support the American system of living. Your commitment in this paragraph will be an accurate measure of your character; therefore, be generous in your assumption of responsibility to your country. Remember, too, that your "mental attitude" toward your country will reflect, to a surprising degree, the "mental attitude" you will display in connection with your closest associates and those to whom you render the service you expect to give in return for the material riches or other type of achievement which you expect. To be respected and well liked by others is the equivalent of removing most of the obstacles that you will find between you and the object of your definite major purpose. You have, therefore, a very sound self-interest reason for improving your relationship with all with whom you become closely associated.

(e) In the fifth paragraph, write out a clear statement of the ways and means you intend to adopt to develop and use the spiritual forces at your command. This commitment on your part may assume any method you desire, but it surely obligates you to follow definite religious habits aimed at a broader and more positive use of your spiritual estate. If you belong to a church, you should intensify and improve your relationship with your spiritual advisers. If you do not belong to a church, and follow no religious learning, you should make such an affiliation. The church provides an atmosphere of spiritual stimulation which every person needs. But here, as in all other human relationships, one can get only in proportion as one gives. The best portion of any church benefit comes from the part one takes in connection with the church activities. Get into harness.

(f) In the sixth paragraph, commit yourself to exercise your right and your duty to vote in all elections in which you are eligible to vote. You cannot be a good citizen without doing your part in choosing dependable and honest public officials. If the spirit of Americanism of which we boast is to remain a free and democratic power for the good of all its citizens, every citizen must assume his full duty in the matter of helping to keep honest men in office, through the power of the ballot.

(g) In the seventh paragraph, write out a clear, definite description of the "mental attitude" in which you intend to improve your relationship with the members of your family. This instruction is of especial importance to men who are the heads of families. A man's wife is, if he relates himself to her properly, of great benefit in helping him to maintain and use his courage. She should be the most important member of his mastermind group, but she will do more harm than good if she is not in full sympathy with his aims and purposes. The fact that a majority of the great leaders, all back through the ages, have had back of them the harmonious cooperation of a woman is profoundly significant. When the minds of a man and his wife are blended in a spirit of continuous harmony, sympathy and oneness of purpose, they can surmount almost any obstacle that may get in their way.

(h) In the eighth paragraph, commit yourself, definitely and irrevocably, never to slander or to speak disparagingly of another person, no matter what may be your impulses to do so. Nothing is more fatal to the development of one's spiritual state than the habit of gossip, small talk, and the slandering of other people. Successful people do not engage in this vulgar habit. It is an insult to one's own soul, a thrust at Infinite Intelligence.

Some men who helped to make america, through the principle of definiteness

As a fitting climax for this chapter, I here present a few brief sketches of some of the well-known men who have contributed to the spirit of Americanism, as we, of this generation, understand that spirit. The records of the achievements of these men show clearly that they understood and applied the principle of Definiteness of Purpose without which, doubtlessly, they could not have been included in this list of distinguished successes.

Henry Ford, America's number one industrialist, although he rates very high on most principles of the philosophy of achievement, has as his greatest distinguishing feature the habit of moving with Definiteness of Purpose. To his application of this principle can be traced, more than to any of the other principles of success, his industrial supremacy and his fortune. Mr. Ford has permitted engineers to streamline his automobiles, but not so with his business policy. From the very beginning of his industrial career, he adopted as his Definite Major Purpose the manufacture and the sale of a dependable, low-priced automobile. That still is his major purpose, and no one will question its soundness, in view of the forty year record of success back of it.

More than two hundred other men, whose names are not now remembered by most people, have come and gone in the business of making automobiles since Henry Ford started in that business. Many of these men had better educations than Mr. Ford, and nearly all of them had more working capital than he, with which to begin their industrial careers. What they did not have, and what they needed more than working capital, was a clear, well-defined spirit of Definiteness of Purpose.

Thomas A. Edison was great because he had a mind that worked with Definiteness of Purpose. Any man who sticks to one task through ten thousand failures, as Edison did in his search for a workable principle for the incandescent electric lamp, could be described with no other adjective than "great." People who are not great generally give up the ghost and quit after but one or two failures, and some even anticipate failure before it arrives and run to cover rather than face it.

When **Walter Chrysler**, as a young man, spent his last dollars for an automobile, he took the machine home to take it apart. He removed every nut, bolt, and screw. He lifted out the pistons and the crankshaft. He removed the valves and the timing gears. Then he went to work and put it all back together again. Over and over again he repeated this performance, until at last his relatives began to think he had lost his mind. But Chrysler knew what he was about! He had chosen, as his Definite Major Purpose, the making of automobiles. Before going into the business he wanted to learn all he could about the mechanical construction of automobiles. But, more important than this, he wanted to make his own mind automobile-conscious. When he finally swung into action and began to build automobiles, his sudden rise to fame and fortune became the talk of the industrial world.

It has been said that a man can have anything he wants if he knows exactly what he wants and desires it badly enough. This seems like a broad claim, but observation of the powers of the mind appear to back it up. A great many years ago **Russell Conwell** wanted a large sum of money with which to found a college in Philadelphia. Having no money of his own, and not knowing where to turn to acquire it from others through the orthodox commercial channels, he finally was forced to turn to his "inner self," where he influenced his mind to produce an idea that he exchanged for the money he needed. The idea was handed over to him, through a "hunch" that struck his brain with such force that it awakened him from sleep. The idea was simple. It consisted of a lecture he was inspired to write, which he delivered under the title of "Acres of Diamonds." The lecture was delivered by Dr. Conwell many thousands of times, and yielded, during his life-time, an income of over four million dollars. It was later published in book form and it became a best-seller for many years. It is still published.

The lecture seems elementary and simple enough, when it is read from the printed pages of a book, but it has in it the full spiritual force of the great enthusiast who wrote it, and it was this spiritual element which caused it to penetrate the hearts of all who heard the lecture. Whether a man writes a book, preaches a sermon, or builds a motor car, if he draws freely upon the forces of his spiritual estate while he is at work, and knows precisely what he wishes to accomplish through his work, he will be more than apt to turn out a masterpiece. Half-hearted efforts produce nothing but half-finished products. The "mental attitude" in which a man does his work is the determining factor as to its quality. That is why a man does best that which he likes best to do.

Frank Gunsaulus, a young preacher, longed to found a college in Chicago. Being without funds and without influential friends through whom he might procure money, he turned like Dr. Russell Conwell to the "inner self" for his needs. The amount he required was the huge sum of one million dollars, quite a tidy sum for a young, unknown clergyman to procure, single-handed. But "God works in a mysterious way, His wonders to perform."

The Reverend Gunsaulus wanted the million dollars badly enough to cause him to become determined to get it. Starting with nothing but an idea based on a Definite Major Purpose, he sat down in his study and began to concentrate his thoughts upon ways and means of acquiring the fortune he needed. For more than three hours, he never took his mind off that subject. He demanded from his subconscious mind that it project itself into the great reservoir of Infinite Intelligence, where he knew there was no shortage of power to produce money or anything else human beings desire or need, and that it bring him the plan by which he might acquire the money. His disciplined mind went to work for him with speed and accuracy. Disciplined minds always work in this manner.

Within a few hours the answer came. It flashed into his mind out of thin air, as he expressed it. The idea consisted of a sermon he was inspired to prepare, entitled "What I would Do with a Million Dollars." Through the Chicago newspapers, he announced he would preach the following Sunday morning on this subject. The announcement came to the attention of the packing house king, the late Philip D. Armour, who, perhaps out of curiosity (the Reverend Gunsaulus attributed the strange phenomenon to another and providential cause), went to hear the sermon.

After the Reverend Gunsaulus had delivered his sermon, Mr. Armour arose from his seat, walked slowly down the aisle to the pulpit, and to the astonishment of the congregation, reached up and shook hands with the young preacher, and said, "I was greatly impressed by your sermon. If you will come to my office tomorrow morning, I will give you my check for the million dollars you desire." He provided the money and Gunsaulus used it to found the Armour Institute of Technology, one of the well-known colleges of the Middle West.

Gunsaulus told how he went about drawing on his spiritual estate for the answer to his needs. "Before I went into the pulpit to preach that sermon," he explained, "I went into my bathroom, turned out the lights, got on my knees and prayed, for one hour, that my sermon would bring the million dollars I needed. I didn't undertake to tell God where to get the money. I only asked that He guide me to the right source. As I walked into the pulpit, a great feeling of assurance came over me. I felt, then, that I already had the money."

A subsequent comparison of notes between the Reverend Gunsaulus and Mr. Armour revealed the astounding fact that at almost the very minute Gunsaulus entered the bath-room to pray Mr. Armour was reading the newspaper announcement of his sermon, and it was while he was praying that Mr. Armour decided to hear the sermon. "There came over me," said Mr. Armour, "a queer feeling that impelled me to get up and go to hear that sermon."

There is something profoundly impressive about such experiences as these—especially when one knows the principals and has every reason to believe their testimony. Is it not strange, indeed, that men seek their needs hither and yon, only to discover at long last that the real method of approach to the source of supply consists of the only thing over which human beings have full control and that is the power of their own minds? Here is the source of all riches, the answer to all desires, the solution to all problems, yet we often turn to this source only as a last resort, after we have all but killed our spiritual powers through disappointments growing out of our efforts in seeking our needs in other directions.

Knut Hamsun, a young Norwegian, spent twenty years of his life trying to find his place in the world. He had a desire to become successful in some calling, but everything he tried turned out to be a "flop." He accepted such menial jobs as he could find, and was kicked around from place to place. Finally, he secured a job as a street-car conductor in Chicago. The job lasted but a few weeks after which he was summarily discharged. The man who discharged him told him he did not have brains enough to accept nickels from people when they handed the money to him. This challenge aroused Hamsun and caused him to reach a decision to do something which brought about his emancipation from poverty. He sat down on the sidewalk and meditated for several hours, and began, unconsciously at first, to apply the principle of Definiteness of Purpose. He reasoned that whereas he had been the world's most pronounced failure, he would write a book in which he would describe the feelings of a man who enjoyed such "distinction." He called the book *Hunger*, quickly followed by the epic book *Growth of the Soil*. He was awarded the Nobel Prize of $25,000 for literary achievement, and thereafter retired to his beloved Norway, where the publishers of the world made a beaten pathway to his door. He, too, turned to the "inner self," after every other source had failed him and found there a rich goldmine he did not know he possessed.

Milo C. Jones, of Wisconsin, was stricken with double paralysis, and could not move a muscle in his body. Before being afflicted, he was a farmer who made a bare living. When his "misfortune" overtook him, he could no longer work on his farm. Accordingly, out of sheer necessity he turned to the "inner self," discovered his own mind, and started to use it. Lying flat on his back in bed he directed his family in carrying out an idea that came to him as a "hunch" after he became paralyzed. The idea was simple enough. It consisted of raising corn and hogs and converting them into sausage. He called his product "Little Pig Sausage." Before he died, several years afterward, he had amassed a fortune of more than a million dollars, and had established a business that served people throughout the United States.

How strange it is that men do not discover the power of their own minds before they are forced, through affliction or failure, to do so. In his hour of greatest despair, Milo C. Jones discovered his spiritual estate. He drew upon that estate because he had nothing else on which to draw. He told the author that it had never occurred to him, prior to his affliction, to depend upon his mind for his needs. He had been depending upon his hands and legs, a source of supply worth but a few dollars a day at best, overlooking, entirely, the riches of his spiritual estate.

James J. Hill built the Great Northern Railroad system with Definiteness of Purpose and made of it a great success. His rise from the lowly position of telegraph operator to the position of directing head of this system was systematically planned. At no time did he rely upon luck for the acquisition of personal power.

How long will it be until we will learn that people move to one side and make room for the man who knows exactly where he is going and shows by his actions he is determined to get there? But this is true. Test it for yourself and be convinced. Start down the street through a crowd, walking slowly as if you do not know where you are going, with indecision clearly written on your face, and observe how rudely people will push you to one side. Reverse your tactics, quicken your step, look straight ahead and carry a look of determination in your face; then observe how quickly people move out of your way and let you go by. Any crowd will make room for the man who is definitely going somewhere and whose actions indicate definitely he expects people to get out of his way.

The crowded street is not the only place where people will step aside when a man with Definiteness of Purpose showing in his face and actions passes. Any person engaged in the business of selling knows that his own "mental attitude" is a strong deciding factor in making sales. The salesman who approaches his prospective buyer in a doubtful frame of mind somehow projects his frame of mind to the buyer, who picks it up, acts upon it, and refuses to buy. It is a well-known fact that salesmen who know exactly what they want, and are determined to get it, take millions of dollars away from the public annually in return for worthless pieces of paper. It is an equally well-known fact that other salesmen, with less determination and self-assurance, come home empty-handed, although they offer commodities of unquestionable merit and value.

Definiteness of Purpose is a resistless force, no matter how or for what purpose it is used.

In reading the works of **Thomas Paine**, I came upon this very significant statement: "By far the better part of such useful knowledge as I have acquired flashed into my mind following deep meditation and thought." This is the testimony of the man who was credited with being a strong factor in starting the American Revolution.

While organizing the philosophy of individual achievement, in collaboration with **Andrew Carnegie**, the author had the good fortune to be privileged to study, for three and a half years, under the distinguished scientist, **Dr. Elmer R. Gates**, of Chevy Chase, Maryland. I learned from close association with Dr. Gates that the majority of patents which he procured on useful inventions were uncovered through the principle of Definiteness of Purpose.

The method by which these discoveries (some of them basic) were made is as follows: Dr. Gates seated himself at a table in a dark, sound-proof room, concentrated his mind upon such known facts as he possessed in connection with the inventions on which he worked, waited until his mind began to send over new information to him; then he switched on the lights and wrote whatever came into his mind. He earned his living by "sitting" for ideas in this manner, for some of the largest corporations in America, who paid him a fat sum per hour, whether he got desired results or not.

This is an authentic description of the methods of a great scientist. The basis of his procedure was Definiteness of Purpose, through concentration of his mind.

How tragic (but it is true!) that most of us spend the major portion of our lives searching for some idea or plan by which we hope to achieve success, without recognizing that the secret of all success is in our own minds. To draw upon this endless source of power, we have but to take possession of our minds and use them. We of America need nothing of a material nature that we do not already possess in great abundance. We have liberty and freedom such as exists nowhere else. We have undeveloped riches of every conceivable nature. We have great educational institutions and libraries wherein may be had, for the asking, all the worthwhile knowledge that mankind has acquired throughout the history of civilization. We have the greatest industrial system available anywhere. We have the right to use our own initiative in whatever occupation or calling we choose. We have a religious background which offers powers unlimited and full freedom of worship. In brief, we have everything except a well-defined understanding of the power of our own minds; this, unfortunately for those who lack it, is the thing we need most, and paradoxically as it may seem, the thing that costs nothing but the effort to appropriate and use it.

The responsibility of benefiting by this chapter is now yours! Your success or failure in appropriating and benefiting by the principles described in this lesson is inseparably bound up in nine words— positive, dynamic, inspiring words. They are Definiteness, Decision, Determination, Persistence, Courage, Hope, Faith, Initiative, and Repetition. Repeat the words in which you state your Definite Major Purpose over and over again. Make the object of your major purpose in life your obsession. Think about it during every idle moment throughout the day, and never let a day pass without doing something, no matter how little, that will lead you nearer the realization of your goal. Mere repetition of your Definite Major Purpose is not enough. You may repeat it the remainder of your life and avail yourself nothing unless you back your words with action, action, action, and still more action. It is the doing, not the knowing, that counts in life.

If you do not have the proper tools, or the working capital, or the personal associates needed in the full realization of your major purpose, go to work anyway, right where you stand, and you will be surprised when you learn how, in some mysterious manner you may not understand, better tools will be placed in your hands.

Remember, no one is ever thoroughly ready to undertake anything. Always there is something missing, or the time seems to be not quite right. Successful men do not wait for the time to begin a task to be entirely right. They start wherever they happen to be; they take the curves of their course when they reach them, never minding the obstacles they may encounter around the curve, beyond their immediate range of vision. Those who wait for all the equipment needed before making a start never experience success, because complete equipment is seldom available in the beginning of any person's plan.

When asked for the secret of his success, after his triumph over powerful enemies who were trying to destroy him, Disraeli, who was perhaps the greatest Prime Minister Great Britain ever had, replied, "The secret of success is constancy of purpose." This is a fitting thought with which to end this chapter on Definiteness of Purpose.

□

Chapter Two

The Master Mind Principle

Before you read this chapter, you should know that the Master Mind principle is the basis of all personal power that attains noteworthy proportions, in every calling. Throughout the analysis of more than 500 distinguished Americans, whose achievements covered many fields of business and industry, this principle was found to be the very foundation of their successes.

The Master Mind principle probably is the most essential of the principles of this philosophy, for the reason, as Mr. Carnegie has so adequately stated, that it is the medium by which one may borrow the education, experience, and influence of others. Through the application of this principle, Thomas A. Edison, handicapped as he was by lack of even an elementary schooling, became America's greatest inventor. Henry Ford used it to develop his industrial empire throughout America and many other parts of the world.

Andrew Carnegie said that if he were compelled to choose but one of the principles of achievement, and risk his entire chances of success or failure on that one principle, he would choose the Master Mind. A careful analysis of the records of many successful men shows clearly that their achievements were based mainly upon two of the success principles, the Master Mind and Definiteness of Purpose. It would be difficult for anyone to rise above mediocrity without having established a definite goal, through the principle covered by chapter one; but, having chosen an objective, one might attain it only with the aid of the Master Mind principle, by using the intelligence of others.

Before turning this lesson over to Mr. Carnegie, it may help you to follow his analysis of the Master Mind principle if we define this principle as, "An alliance of two or more minds, coordinated and working together in a spirit of perfect harmony, for the attainment of a definite purpose."

From this definition, it is obvious that a Master Mind alliance may consist of two people, working in harmony for the achievement of some special purpose; or it may consist of any number that may be required, according to the nature of the purpose to be accomplished.

Observe, with profit, the emphasis on the word "harmony," the reason for which will become clear as you read what Mr. Carnegie has to say on this subject. I take you now, to the private study of the great steel-master, where you may sit in while he describes the principle to which he gives credit for the major portion of his astounding achievements.

Carnegie: Definiteness of Purpose is the first of the Principles of Achievement. The second of these principles is the Master Mind. No one can hope to become successful without having first decided what he wants; but the mere choice of a major purpose in life is not, of itself, enough to ensure success. To achieve the object of one's major goal, if it be of proportions above mediocrity, one must have the help and the education and the experience of others.

Moreover, one must so relate himself to the members of his Master Mind alliance that he will procure the full benefit of their brains, in a spirit of harmony! Failure to understand the importance of harmony and sympathy of purpose in the mind of every member of a Master Mind alliance has cost many men their chances of success in business.

A man may bring together a group of men whose cooperation he appears to have, and perhaps on the surface he will have it; but the thing that counts is not surface appearances; it is the "mental attitude" of each member of the group. Before any alliance of men can constitute a Master Mind every man in the group must have his heart as well as his head in full sympathy with the object of the alliance, and he must be in perfect harmony with his leader and every other member of the alliance.

Hill: I believe I understand your point, Mr. Carnegie, but I do not see how a man can ever be sure of inducing his associates, in a Master Mind alliance, to work with him in complete harmony. Will you explain how this is accomplished?

Carnegie: Yes, I can tell you exactly how harmonious relations are established and maintained. To begin with, remember that everything a man does has back of his action a definite motive. We are all creatures of habit and motive. We begin doing things because of a motive; we continue doing them because of both motive and habit, but there may come a time when motive is forgotten and we continue on because of established habit.

There are but nine major motives to which people respond. I will describe these, then you will see for yourself how men are influenced to work with others in a spirit of harmony. At the very outset, in the organization of a Master Mind group, the leader must select, as individual members of his alliance, first: men who have the ability to do what is required of them; and secondly, men who will respond in a spirit of harmony to the particular motive held out to them in return for their aid.

THE NINE MAJOR MOTIVES

Here are the nine motives, some combination of which creates the "moving spirit" back of everything we do:

1. The emotion of love (The gateway to one's spiritual power).
2. The emotion of sex (Purely biological, but may serve as a powerful stimulant to action, when transmuted).
3. Desire for financial gain.
4. Desire for self-preservation.
5. Desire for freedom of body and mind.
6. Desire for self-expression leading to fame, recognition.
7. Desire for perpetuation of life after death.
8. The emotion of anger, often expressed as envy or jealousy.
9. The emotion of fear.

   (The last two motives are negative, but very powerful as stimulants to action).

Here you have the nine major approaches to all minds!

In the successful maintenance of a Master Mind alliance, the leader around whom the alliance is formed must depend upon one or more of these basic motives to induce each member of his group to give the harmonious cooperation required for success.

The two motives to which men respond most generously in business alliances are the emotion of sex and the desire for financial gain. Most men want money more than any other thing; but they often want it mainly to please the woman of their choice. Here, then, the motivating force is three-fold: love, sex, and financial gain.

There is a type of man, however, who will work harder for recognition than he will for material or financial gain. This type of ego may become very powerful, in the attainment of highly constructive objectives, where sufficient self-control is used to ensure harmony.

Hill: From what you say, Mr. Carnegie, it appears that the man who successfully builds an organization of men into a Master Mind alliance must know men quite well. Will you explain how you managed to choose, so successfully, the men in your Master Mind group? Did you pick your men at sight, or did you select them by the trial and error method, replacing those that proved unsuited for the purpose for which they were chosen?

Carnegie: No man is smart enough to judge other men accurately by sight. There are certain surface indications which may be suggestive of a man's ability, but there is one quality which is more important than all others, as the deciding factor of a man's value as a member of a Master Mind alliance, and that, unfortunately, is not a mere surface quality; it is his "mental attitude" toward himself and his associates. If his attitude happens to be negative, and he is inclined to be selfish, egotistical or adversely provocative in his relationship with others, he will not fit into a Master Mind alliance.

Moreover, if such a man is allowed to remain as a member of a Master Mind group he may become so obstructive in his influence with the other members that he will destroy their usefulness as well as his own.

An experience we had in our own Master Mind group, some years ago, will illustrate my meaning. Our Chief Chemist died and we had to find a man to fill his place. We tried out the assistant in the job, but he lacked the experience the job required, so we had to search for an older and more experienced man. We finally located a man in Europe whose record made him appear to be the very man we wanted, but when we came to negotiate with him we discovered that he did not wish to leave Europe. To procure the services of this man, it became necessary to offer him, as the motive to which he was willing to respond, a much larger salary than we had been paying our Chief

Chemist. In addition to this, he demanded a five-year contract. He got what he asked for and we installed him in the job, only to learn very quickly that he was a stubborn, temperamental fellow who could not or would not work harmoniously with the other members of our staff. We tried, without success, to induce him to change his mental attitude. Accordingly, at the end of the first six months of his association with us it became evident that we had to rid ourselves of him, so we paid him off for the full five years and he went back home. The experience was costly, but nothing to compare with what he would have cost us if we had kept him, as a disrupting force, in our Master Mind group.

Our next Chief Chemist was employed on a year's probationary period, with full notice in advance of his employment that harmony was the watch word of our organization.

It is a well-known fact that one man, whose mental attitude is negative, if he is in a position of authority, will project his influence down into the rank and file of an entire organization of men, so changing their mental attitude as to make them dissatisfied and therefore inefficient in their work.

Emerson knew what he was saying when he wrote, "Every institution is the lengthened shadow of one man." Successful men make it their business to watch carefully the sort of "extended shadow" they project. I would change Emerson's statement slightly, by saying that every business is the extended shadow of the men who manage it, for in this day of large organizations it is impossible for one man to become the entire guiding influence of a great industrial enterprise such as the United States Steel Corporation. It would be more correct if we said that this corporation is the extended shadow of the Master Mind that guides it. In this instance, the Master Mind consists of more than a score of individual minds, working together in a spirit of harmony, for the achievement of a definite purpose.

Some of the members of our Master Mind group came up from the rank and file of our workers, after having demonstrated their ability. Some of them were chosen from the outside, through the trial and error method. In most instances, those who came from the outside had established their ability in some other field or occupation, where their records of achievement were sufficiently outstanding to bring them to our attention. Some of the ablest men in our Master Mind group started at the very bottom and worked their way up through many different departments of our industry. These men know the value of harmony and cooperative effort. That is one of the secrets of their ability to promote themselves into high positions. The man who has ability in any line, plus the right mental attitude toward his associates, usually is found at the top of the ladder, no matter what his occupation may be. There is a great premium on efficiency plus the right mental attitude. I wish you would stress this fact in your presentation of the philosophy of individual achievement.

Hill: What about the man who organizes a group of men into a Master Mind alliance? Is it not necessary for him to be a master in the field of endeavour in which he is engaged, before he can successfully manage others in that field?

Carnegie: I can best answer that question by telling you that I, personally, know but little of the technical requirements in manufacturing and marketing of steel; nor is it essential that I have this knowledge. Here is where the Master Mind principle comes to one's aid. I have surrounded myself with more than a score of men whose combined education, experience and ability give me the full benefit of all that is known, up to the present time, about the making and marketing of steel. My job is to keep these men inspired with a desire to do the finest possible job. My method of inspiration can be easily traced right back to the nine basic motives, and especially to the motive of desire for financial gain. I have a system of compensation which permits every member of my Master Mind group to name his own financial reward, but the system is so arranged that beyond a certain maximum salary which each man is allowed, an individual must establish definite proof that he has earned more than this amount before he receives it.

This system encourages individual initiative, imagination, and enthusiasm, and leads to continuous personal development and growth. Under the system I have paid such men as Charlie Schwab as much as a million dollars in one year, over and above the maximum salary scale. It was this system which inspired Schwab to develop his own individual initiative to the point at which he was the major moving spirit in the organization of the great United States Steel Corporation. Along with his initiative he developed great ability as a leader.

Remember, my major purpose in life is the development of men—not merely the accumulation of money. The money I possess came as a natural reward for the efforts I have put into developing men.

I know that some people accuse me of being money-mad, but those who do so know nothing of my major purpose. The best evidence of the true nature of my purpose is the fact that I am giving my money away as rapidly as I can do so without damaging other people, and the better portion of my riches, consisting of the knowledge I have gained in the art of developing men, I am presenting to the world, through your efforts, in the form of a practical philosophy of individual achievement. This is the only way wealth can be fairly and permanently distributed, because true wealth is the product of the mind, a form of riches toward which every material thing gravitates.

Hill: You say that all success, of noteworthy proportions, is the result of understanding and application of the Master Mind principle. Are there not some exceptions to this rule, Mr. Carnegie? Couldn't a man become a great artist, or a great preacher, or a successful salesman, without the use of the Master Mind principle?

Carnegie: The answer to your question, the way you have stated it, is no! A man might become an artist, or a preacher, or a salesman without direct application of the Master Mind principle, but he could not become great in these fields of endeavour without the aid of this principle. An all-wise Providence has so arranged the mechanism of the mind that no single mind is complete. Richness of the mind, in its fullest sense, comes from the harmonious alliance of two or more minds, working toward the achievement of some definite purpose.

For example, the Master Mind that gave this nation its birth of liberty and freedom consisted of a composite mind that grew out of the harmonious alliance of the 56 men who signed the Declaration of Independence. Back of that Master Mind was the Definiteness of Purpose which we, of today, know as the American Spirit of Self-determination, a portion of which has served as the motivating power in the development of our great American industry.

No one mind, no matter how great it might have been, could have given this nation the vision, the initiative, the self-reliance by which its leaders in every walk of life have been inspired.

There are one-man industries, and one-man businesses, but they are not great; and there are individuals who go all the way through life without allying themselves, in a spirit of harmony, with other minds, but they are not great, and their achievements are meager.

Remember you have been assigned the responsibility of giving to the world a complete philosophy of individual achievement; therefore, you must include in the philosophy those factors which enable an individual to rise above mediocrity. The most important of these factors is an understanding of the power that is available to the person who blends his mind-power with that of other people, thereby giving himself the full benefit of an intangible force which no single mind can ever experience.

We live in a great nation. It is great because of the power and the vision of the combined forces of the minds of many people who, working in harmony under our form of government, enable industry and banking and agriculture and private enterprise in every walk of life to put up a solid front. Our form of government is an excellent example of the principle of the Master Mind, combining as it does, the harmonious cooperative effort of both the State and Federal units of government. Under this friendly alliance, we have grown and prospered as no other nation known to civilization has done. Successful businesses become successful because their leaders adopt and use this same principle of friendly alliance between those who manage the businesses.

Come over here to the window and I will show you, out there in the railroad yards, a fine example of the Master Mind in action in transportation. Out there you see a freight train being made ready for its run. The train will be in the charge of a crew of men who coordinate their efforts in a spirit of harmony. The conductor is the leader of the crew. He can take the train to its destination only because all the other members of the crew recognize and respect his authority and carry out his instructions in a spirit of harmony. What do you suppose would happen to that train if the Engineer neglected or refused to obey the Conductor's signals?

Hill: Why, there might be a wreck that would cost the entire crew their lives.

Carnegie: Exactly so! Well, running a business successfully calls for the application of the same Master Mind principle that is so essential in the operation of a railroad train. When there is lack of harmony between those engaged in running a business, the bankruptcy court is not far away. Are you following me in this description? I want you to understand it, because it deals with the very heart of all successful achievement, in every field of human endeavor.

Hill: I understand the Master Mind principle, Mr. Carnegie, although I never thought of it as being the sole source of your stupendous achievements in the steel industry, and the basis of your huge fortune.

Carnegie: Oh no! It is not the sole source of my accomplishments. Other principles have entered into the accumulation of my money, and the building of a great steel industry, but they have been of less importance than the Master Mind. The principle of second importance to the Master Mind is Definiteness of Purpose. These two principles, combined, have produced what the world calls a successful industry. Neither of these, by itself, could have brought success.

Look at those hoboes down there in that freight yard, and you'll see a perfect example of a group of men without either Definiteness of Purpose or a Master Mind. There is also an example of lack of purpose and coordination of effort. If those men would put their heads together and choose a definite purpose, and adopt a definite plan for carrying out their purpose, they might well be the crew that runs that freight train, instead of an unfortunate, poverty-stricken group of homeless men. Do you see what I mean?

Hill: I see well enough, Sir; but how is it that these men were never taught the principles of achievement as you are describing them to me? Why have they not discovered the power of the Master Mind, as you have done?

Carnegie: I did not discover the Master Mind principle, I appropriated it; took it literally from the Bible.

Hill: From the Bible, Sir? Why, I never knew the Bible taught the practical philosophy of achievement. In what portion of the Bible did you find the Master Mind principle?

Carnegie: I found it in the New Testament, in the story of Christ and His Twelve Disciples. You remember the story, of course.

As far as I have been able to learn, Christ was the first person in history who made definite use of the Master Mind principle. You recall Christ's unusual power and the power of His disciples after He was crucified. It is my theory that Christ's power grew out of His relationship with God and that the power of His disciples grew out of their harmonious alliance with Him. I believe that He stated a great truth when He said to His followers that they could perform even greater things, for He had discovered that the blending of two or more minds in a spirit of harmony with a definite end in view, gives one contact with the Universal Mind which is of God. I call your attention to what happened when Judas Iscariot broke faith with Christ. The breaking of the bond of harmony brought the Master the supreme catastrophe of His life, and for the sake of practical paraphrasing may I suggest that when the bond of harmony is broken, for any cause whatsoever, between the members of a Master Mind group that operates a business, or a home, ruination is just around the corner!

If called upon to state your major purpose in life, in one sentence, what would your answer be?

Hill: Can the Master Mind principle be of practical benefit in other than business relationships, Mr. Carnegie?

Carnegie: Oh yes! it can be of practical use in connection with any form of human relationship where cooperation is necessary. Take the home, for example, and observe what happens when a man and his wife and other members of the family put their hearts and heads together and work for the common good of the entire family.

Here you will find happiness, contentment, and financial security. Poverty and misery are attracted by those who neglect to work together in harmony.

You have often heard it said that a man's wife can make or break him!

Well, it is true, and I'll tell you why. The alliance of a man and a woman in marriage creates the most perfect known form of Master Mind, providing the alliance is blended with love, sympathy of understanding, oneness of purpose, and complete harmony. Evidence of this may be found in the fact that one may find the influence of a woman as the major motivating force in the life of practically all the distinguished men of achievement down through the ages. But let misunderstanding and disagreement enter into such an alliance between a man and his wife, and he will become practically helpless in the use of his will power. A man's wife may make or break him because her mind and his become so closely blended in marriage that her virtues become his virtues and her faults become his faults.

Fortunate indeed is the man who is married to a woman who devotes her life to strengthening his own mind power by blending with it her own, in a spirit of sympathetic understanding and harmony. That type of wife will never "break" any man, but she will be most likely to help him rise to greater heights of achievement than any he would have known without her help.

Hill: If I understand you correctly, Mr. Carnegie, a proper application and use of the Master Mind principle gives an individual the benefit of the education and experience of other people, but it goes much beyond this and aids the individual in contacting and using the spiritual forces available to him. Is that your understanding of the principle?

Carnegie: That is precisely my understanding of it. A great psychologist once said that no two minds ever come into contact without there being born, of that association, a third and intangible mind, of greater power than either of the two minds. Whether this third mind becomes a help or a hindrance to one or both of the two contacting minds depends entirely upon the mental attitude of each. If the attitude of both minds is harmonious, sympathetic and cooperative, then the third mind born of the contact may be beneficial to both. If the attitude of one or both of the contacting minds is antagonistic or controversial, unfriendly, the third mind born of the contact will be harmful to both.

The Master Mind principle is no man-made principle, you know. It is a part of the great system of natural law, and it is as immutable as the law of gravitation which holds the stars and planets in their places, and as definite in every phase of its operation. We may not be able to influence this law, but we can understand it and adapt ourselves to it in ways that will bring us great benefits, no matter who we are or what our calling may be.

Two very humble men of my acquaintance found a practical use for the Master Mind. One of them is blind and the other is crippled so that he has lost the use of his legs. One day these two men met and began to tell of their handicaps. The blind man said he was having a very hard time getting along, with people stepping on his toes, and automobiles whizzing by. "You have nothing on me," said the crippled man. "I can see the automobiles, but I can't get out of the way fast enough." Straightening himself up, with a broad grin on his face, the blind man exclaimed that he had an idea which might be of help to both men. "I have a sound pair of legs," said he, "while you have a sound pair of eyes. Now, you climb on my back and use your eyes, while I will supply the legs, and between us we will get along lots faster and much safer."

Everyone, figuratively speaking, is a bit blind or lame in that he needs some form of cooperation from others. The blind man needed only the use of another man's eyes. In the operation of my business, I needed the education and experience of a large corps of men who understood the technical requirements in making and marketing steel. In your work of organizing all of the causes of success and all of the major causes of failure into a new practical philosophy of individual achievement you will need the cooperation of hundreds of men who have succeeded in their chosen fields of endeavor, and the help of many thousands who have tried and failed. Because of the nature of your undertaking you will need to understand and apply the Master Mind principle over a long period of years. Without the aid of this principle you cannot complete the work you are beginning, for there is no one person living who could supply you with all the major causes of both success and failure.

Hill: From your analysis of the Master Mind principle I gather the impression, Mr. Carnegie, that men who have been deprived of an early education need not limit their ambition on that account since it is both possible and practical for them to use the education of others. I also get the impression, from what you have said, that no man ever acquires so much education that he can achieve noteworthy success without the aid of other minds. Is this your understanding?

Carnegie: Both of your statements are correct. Lack of schooling is no valid excuse for failure; neither is an exhaustive schooling a guarantee of success. Someone once said that knowledge is power, but he told only a half truth, for knowledge is only potential power. It may become a power only when it is organized and expressed in terms of definite action! Many young men have done themselves great damage by assuming, upon graduation from college, that their knowledge of academic subjects is sufficient to guarantee them good jobs. There is a big difference between having an abundant stock of knowledge and being educated. The difference will become apparent if you look up the Latin root from which the word educate is derived. The word educate comes from the Latin word educare, which means to draw out, to develop from within, to grow through use. It does not mean to acquire and store knowledge!

Success is the power to get whatever one desires in life, without violating the rights of others. Observe that I used the word power! Knowledge is not power, but the appropriation and use of other men's knowledge and experience, for the attainment of some definite purpose, is power; moreover, it is power of the most beneficial order.

The man who applies the Master Mind principle for the purpose of availing himself of the minds of other men, usually begins by taking complete charge of the power of his own mind! I wish to emphasize the importance of an individual's removing self-imposed limitations which most people set up in their own minds.

In a country like America, where there is an abundance of every form of riches; where every man is free to choose his own occupation and live his own life in his own way; there is no reason why any man should set low limitations on his achievements, nor be satisfied with less than all the material possessions his personal desires need or demand.

In our country, there is a high premium on individual initiative, imagination, and definiteness of purpose, and they are aided by the easy accessibility of the material things each man requires to fulfil his idea of success. Here a man may be born in poverty, but he does not have to go through life in poverty. He may be illiterate, but he does not have to remain so. But here, as in every other part of the world, no amount of opportunity will benefit the man who neglects or refuses to take possession of his own mind power and use it to his own personal advancement.

For the sake of emphasis, I repeat that no man can take the fullest possession of his own mind power without combining it, through the Master Mind principle, with the minds of others, for the attainment of a definite purpose.

Hill: Inasmuch as you have commissioned me to give the world a practical philosophy of individual achievement, will you outline for me step by step a complete plan which one should follow in the organization of a Master Mind group? This procedure is not quite clear to me; it may be less so to the person who has had no experience in the use of the Master Mind principle.

Carnegie: The procedure in every individual case would be slightly different, depending on the education, experience, personality, and mental attitude of the person starting to organize a Master Mind group, and the purpose for which he is organizing it; but in every instance there are certain fundamentals to be observed, some of the most important of which are as follows:

(a) *Definiteness of Purpose* – The starting point in all achievement is definite knowledge of what one wants. Under this classification one should follow the formula laid down in chapter one, carrying out every detail of those instructions to the letter.

(b) *Choosing members for a master mind group* – Every person with whom an individual allies himself, under the Master Mind principle, should be in complete sympathy with the object of the alliance, and must be able to contribute something definite toward the attainment of that object. The contribution may consist of the member's education, experience, or, as is so often the case, it may consist of the use of the goodwill he has established in his relationship with the public, commonly known as "contacts." Many banks and other corporations add to their Master Mind groups many high-priced men who serve no purpose other than to provide the corporation with the use of the goodwill and public influence they carry.

(c) *Motive* – No one has the right, and seldom does anyone have the ability, to induce others to serve as members of their Master Mind group, without giving something in return for the service they receive. The motive may be financial reward, or it may consist of some form of return favours, but it must be something which is of equal value to or greater than the service expected. In my own Master Mind alliance, as I have stated, the motive used to induce full and harmonious cooperation from some of the members of my group was financial reward. I helped some of the members of my alliance—those who had the ability to earn it—to earn more money by far than they could have made through any sort of effort independent of me. I believe it is no exaggeration to say that every member of my Master Mind group made a more practical an profitable use of his individual ability, in alliance with me, than he would have done if he had worked independently. I cannot overemphasize the fact that the man who tries to build a Master Mind alliance without determining that every member of his alliance profits in proportion to his value in the alliance is doomed to certain failure.

(d) *Harmony* – Complete harmony must prevail among all members of a Master Mind alliance, if success is to be ensured. There can be no "behind the back" disloyalties on the part of any member of the group. Every member of the alliance must subordinate his own personal opinions, his own desires for personal advancement for the fullest benefit of the group as a whole, by thinking only in terms of the successful achievement of the object of the alliance. In the choice of individuals to serve as allies in a Master Mind group, first consideration should be given to the question as to whether or not the individual can and will work for the good of the group. Any member who is unable to do this must, upon discovery of his deficiency, be replaced by someone who can and will do so. There can be no compromise on this point, a fact which often will automatically exclude one's relatives and closest personal friends who, unfortunately, cannot subordinate their personal ego for any purpose.

(e) *Action* – Once formed, a Master Mind group must become and remain active to be effective. The group must move on a definite plan, at a definite time, toward a definite end. Indecision, inaction or delay will destroy the usefulness of the entire group. Moreover, there is an old saying that the best way to keep a mule from kicking is to keep him so busy pulling he will have neither the time nor the inclination to kick. The same may be said about men. I have seen sales organizations die of dry rot because the man in charge of the organization allowed his men to come and go as they pleased, without giving them definite quotas to attain. Lack of a definite plan for budgeting and using time is the greatest evil of all salesmen who work on a commission basis, such as Life Insurance salesmen. Success in any undertaking calls for definite, well-organized, and continuous work! Nothing has yet been invented to take the place of work! Not all the brains of the world are sufficient to enable a man to achieve outstanding success without work.

(f) *Leadership* – Do not imagine that the mere selection of a group of men who agree to work together in a spirit of harmony, for the achievement of a definite purpose, is sufficient to ensure the success of their efforts. The leader who organizes the group must actually lead. As far as work is concerned he should be the first to arrive at the place of work, and the last to leave; moreover, he should set his associates a good example by doing as much or more work than they. The greatest of all "Bosses" is the man who makes himself the most nearly indispensable, and not the man who happens to have the last word when decisions are to be made and plans are to be chosen. Every leader's motto should be "The Greatest among You shall be the Servant of All!"

(g) *Mental Attitude* – In a Master Mind alliance, as in all other human relationships, the factor which, more than all others, determines the extent and nature of the cooperation one gets from others is his own mental attitude. I can say truthfully that in my relationship with my own Master Mind group there never was a time when I did not hope that every man in the alliance would get from the alliance the fullest possible measure of personal benefit; and there never was a time when I did not try, with all the resources of what ability I possessed, to develop in every member of my alliance the fullest potentialities of his own ability. I believe this attitude on my part was the strongest factor in the development of men like Charlie Schwab, who earned as much as a million dollars a year over and above their regular salaries. I could have had the services of such men as Schwab, without being compelled to pay such high bonuses for extraordinary achievements; but I would have deprived myself of the benefits of that sort of service, because I would have destroyed the motive which prompted them to render it.

One of the most beautiful sights on earth, and one of the most inspiring, is that of a group of men who work together in a spirit of perfect harmony, each man thinking only in terms of what he can do for the benefit of the group. It was this spirit that gave almost superhuman power to the ragged, underfed, under clothed armies of George Washington, in their fight against the overwhelming odds of better equipped soldiers. These men were fighting for a common cause, and not for personal aggrandizement alone. Wherever one finds an employer and his employees working together in this spirit of mutual helpfulness, one finds a successful organization.

One of the major benefits of athletic training is that it tends to teach men to do teamwork in a spirit of harmony! What a pity that after leaving school men do not always carry with them into their jobs this same spirit of teamwork. I have often wished I might organize all the workers in my steel plants into a gigantic two-teamgroup of men who would devote an hour each day to friendly opposition, through some form of athletics that would inspire them with the spirit of teamwork. It would help them overcome intolerance, envy, and selfishness, and improve them in other ways that would make them worth more to the business and more to themselves inside and outside of their jobs. Life is less burdensome to the man who has the spirit of good sportsmanship in his make-up. Therefore, let the spirit of sportsmanship become an important factor in every undertaking based on the Master Mind principle, and let it begin with the man who organizes the group. The others will get the spirit from his example.

(h) *Confidential Relationship* – The relationship existing between men, under the Master Mind principle, should be a confidential one. The purpose of the alliance should never be discussed outside of the ranks of the members unless the object of the alliance is that of performing some public service. There are people who take keen delight in placing obstacles in the way of those who are working for personal achievement. Such people can do little harm if they do not understand what is the purpose of one's Master Mind alliance. The best of all possible ways of telling the world what one is going to do is by showing the world what one has already done. Publicity, press notices and the like have great value at times, but they may do great harm if they disclose the nature of one's unachieved plans.

Be careful what you set your heart upon, for you may live to see yourself in possession of it.

I have heard it said that every very great man—and there are a few such men during every generation—always has some aims and purposes in his mind which are known to no one except himself and his God. Perhaps you may not aspire to be great, but you may profit greatly if you bear this statement in mind and refrain from announcing your aims and plans prior to their fulfillment. It is always more satisfying to say "I have accomplished my aim" than it is to say "I am going to do thus and so, if and when I get around to it." The personal pronoun goes much better with the past tense than it does with the future tense.

It is astounding to learn to what extent some men will go to give away the vital trade secrets of their business, to whomsoever will listen, because of their love of idle self-expression. In this manner, employees often disclose important business and trade secrets of their employers. The desire for self-expression is one of the nine basic motives which move men to action, but it can become a dangerous habit if not used with discretion. The smartest people who indulge their desire for self-expression usually do so by asking questions instead of answering questions for others. This is one way to give full play to the desire for self-expression without self-injury.

Hill: Mr. Carnegie, will you describe what you believe to be the most important Master Mind alliance in the United States, and give some idea of how it operates?

Carnegie: The most important Master Mind alliance in America, or for that matter in the entire world, is the alliance between the states of our country. From this alliance comes the freedom and liberty of which we in America feel so proud. The strength of the alliance lies in the fact that it is voluntary and that in a spirit of harmony it is supported by the people. The alliance between the States has created a greater variety of opportunities for the exercise of individual initiative than exists anywhere else in the whole world. Moreover, it has created the necessary power to defend its people and the system under which it operates, against all who may envy us or desire to interfere with our privileges.

Our entire system (including our form of government, our industrial plan, our banking institution, and our life insurance system) was designed and is maintained as a favourable medium for the support of private enterprise and as an encouragement to personal initiative. It is the greatest system in the world because it is so designed and maintained that it provides the simplest and best of all possible media for the free and undisturbed expression of individual effort based on the nine basic motives.

The Master Mind principle under which our country is operated is so flexible and democratic that it can be modified, changed, or improved at will to meet the needs of changing times. It serves as a dependable pattern by which individuals or corporations desiring to adopt the Master Mind principle can be safely guided. When our Master Mind alliance becomes inadequate for our needs, in any respect whatsoever, the people who formed it can improve it by the simple process of voting an amendment to our Constitution.

If all employers and employees related themselves to one another under a Master Mind plan similar to the one under which our country is operated, there would be no occasion for serious misunderstanding between them. Moreover, both the employer and the employees would receive more benefits from their joint efforts. There could be, and there should be, a pure democracy as the basis of all relationships between employers and employees, the same as there is a pure democracy on which the relationship between the States of America is based.

The operating principle of the Master Mind alliance under which our country is managed is simple. It consists of a triumvirate known as the executive, the judiciary, and the legislative bodies, all working in a spirit of harmony, in direct response to the will of the people. This system is used in the management of the individual States, as well as in the management of the entire alliance of States known as the Federal Government. The system can be changed by the will of the people, and the public officials who administer the system can, with very few rare exceptions, be retired on short notice. So far no better system of human relationship has been found, and no better system is in the prospect of being found within the near future. Perhaps no better system than ours will ever be found and none will be necessary as long as our present system is managed as its founders intended it should be managed for the greatest possible benefits to all, with special privileges for none.

Hill: Can you think of any improvements the people of America could make in their present form of government, Mr. Carnegie?

Carnegie: I can think of no improvements they might make in their form of government, but I can name one very great improvement they might make in their method of administering their government, and that would be the passing of a law requiring all eligible voters to vote in all local and national elections, under the penalty of heavy fines for failure to vote. If our form of government ever ceases to serve us adequately, it will be because of the negligence of the people in not voting. Already I can see great abuses of public office due to the failure of people to concern themselves about the election of dependable men. This form of neglect is an open bid to dishonest men to grab the reins of government, as some have done in such cities as New York and Chicago, where individual interest and civic pride are lacking.

I can think of one other improvement that might be made in connection with our method of choosing public office-holders, and that would be a system through which the personal records of all candidates for public office would have to be adequately published so all voters could judge a candidate's fitness for office. Under our present system, the only publicity the voters see, in connection with a candidate's personal record, is that which the candidates themselves publish concerning themselves or their opponents, and this is none too reassuring in most instances. A third improvement which might be made that would aid the people in a wise choice of candidates for public office, would consist of a course of training through which the people would be taught, in the public schools, how to choose candidates best fitted to serve them.

Successful business men do not employ men to fill responsible positions without enquiring into the applicant's personal record. They look into the ability of the man whom they employ to do the job for which he is chosen, and they also investigate his character. The same procedure should be followed in selecting men to fill public office.

Hill: You made some brief reference to application of the Master Mind principle as a medium for the successful operation of the home, Mr. Carnegie. Will you go further into this subject and explain just how this principle can be applied in the management of the home?

Carnegie: I am glad you thought of this, because my experience has taught me that a man's home relationship has an important bearing on his business or professional achievements. Now I want you to remember that my remarks on this subject will be general, and not intended as a guide in all cases.

The alliance between a man and a woman in marriage creates a relationship which reaches deeply into the spiritual nature of both parties. For this reason, marriage provides the most favourable of all human alliances for the effective use of the Master Mind principle.

In marriage, as in all other relationships, there are certain precautions one can take to ensure the successful operation of the Master Mind principle. The more important of these safeguards is:

(a) *The Choice of a Mate* – A successful marriage begins with an intelligent choice of a partner. Let me explain what I mean by an intelligent choice. In the first place, inasmuch as a man usually does the choosing (or at least thinks he does), he should test his prospective partner in marriage through a series of very frank and intimate talks with her, covering at least the fundamentals of a marriage relationship.

He should tell her how he intends to make a living and be very sure she is in full accord with him, both as to his chosen occupation and his methods of following it. It is all very well to talk of love, and romance, and the aesthetic side of life, when a man is selling himself to the woman of his choice; but he should not forget that there is a very practical, and a somewhat prosaic side to marriage, and this side of marriage begins to make its appearance at about the time the honeymoon begins to cool down. So, the sensible thing for a man to do is to anticipate the practical realities of marriage and reach an understanding with his prospective wife concerning them, well in advance of their arrival.

It will be of priceless help to a man if his wife becomes so thoroughly sold on his occupation, and his method of earning his living, that her interest may be described as intensely enthusiastic; but her minimum interest in this very important fundamental of the partnership of marriage should be an unreserved approval of his occupation. Failure to have an understanding on this important subject has destroyed the possibility of application of the Master Mind principle in many marriages. If a man's wife is more interested in a game of bridge than she is in her husband's source of income, he may as well look in some other direction for his Master Mind cooperation. Sometimes this is exactly what a man does. Let the wives of men remember this! If a woman is really very smart, she will take this suggestion and carry it through to its logical climax, through the aid of her own imagination.

I have observed several instances where a man and his wife were engaged in the same occupation, or the same business, and worked together for the attainment of a common purpose. In every such circumstance, I was impressed by the fact that their close association in occupation led also to a close relationship in their social affairs, which left very little surplus time for either of them to become interested in anything or anyone that did not concern both.

There is another advantage of vital importance to both a man and his wife in their having a mutual interest in the source of their income, and that is the fact that this leads to a mutual understanding regarding their household and personal expenditures. If a man's wife knows precisely how he makes his money, and how much he makes, she will, if she is a faithful partner, adjust her household and personal expenditures to fit his income; moreover, she will do it cheerfully. I have known of more than one marriage to go on the rocks because the wife made financial demands upon her husband which he could not meet, and I have known of more than one husband who was driven to dishonesty in his struggle to satisfy his spendthrift wife.

So far I have been speaking for the benefit of the man who has not chosen a life partner in marriage. "But what about the man who is already married?" Some will ask. "What can he do if he has chosen a wife who has no interest in his occupation, or perhaps no common interest with him on any subject? Have you no remedy to offer this man?"

Yes, there is a remedy for most cases of this sort, and it consists of a reselling job on the husband's part, with the object of inducing the wife to begin all over again, under a plan that will ensure closer cooperation between them. There are but few marriages which do not need a new and improved plan of relationship at frequent intervals, to ensure the fullest measure of benefits to both parties to the marriage and to their children where there are children.

Success in marriage calls for continuous vigilance on the part of both parties, with the object of avoiding misunderstandings through a carefully planned relationship affecting all members of the family. The time would be well spent if married people set aside a regular hour for a confidential Master Mind meeting at least once every week, during which they would come to an understanding concerning every vital factor of their relationship, both in and outside of the home association. Continuous contact between men engaged in the management of a business is an essential for harmony and cooperative effort. It is no less essential between a man and his wife.

The United States Navy follows a rule which might well be adopted in every home. It is a requirement that every ship of a Naval Fleet communicate with the Flagship hourly, whether there is anything to report or not. Contact is all important! It is just as important in the management of a home as it is in the operation of the United States Navy. Taking things for granted, without mutual agreement between a man and his wife, is the beginning of loss of interest in one another. The Master Mind principle cannot be successfully applied in marriage without a deliberate, carefully planned program for its application. An occasional discussion of the mutual affairs of marriage is not enough. There must be an established period set aside for Master Mind relationships, and this portion of the marriage program should be respected and carried out with the same courtesy, the same Definiteness of Purpose, and the same formality that is observed by business men who use the Master Mind principle for the management of their affairs.

Fortunate, indeed, will be the mates in marriage who heed this counsel and make the fullest possible use of it in the management of their alliance, for they are sure to discover in it an approach to perfection in marriage which can never be attained through mere physical attraction or sex emotion.

A sound partnership in marriage must include understanding and harmony of purpose in connection with the source of the income that supports the home. The income should be budgeted so that both a man and his wife may have equal access to it. The man who forces his wife to go through his pockets after he goes to sleep at night for the purpose of stealing spending money she wishes to use for her own private purposes, will never hold her respect nor will she be of much help to him as a Master Mind ally.

A partnership in marriage should include a joint interest and joint ownership in every material thing owned by both partners! The man who believes he can keep his business affairs to himself, without taking his wife into his full confidence, may as well recognize that if he follows this policy there can be no application of the Master Mind principle in his home affairs. Of course, there are instances where a man's wife, through lack of interest in her husband's affairs, or an irritable disposition, forces him to keep his own counsel. In a case of this nature, the only remedy is that of the renaissance of the mutual interests of the two which brought them together and led to their marriage. Here one should take warning that if this revival of mutual interest is delayed or neglected for very long, the job may prove difficult.

Hill: Your impression, then, seems to indicate that you believe the future of America holds as many opportunities as any that were available to you in the past. Is that correct?

Carnegie: You have understated my belief! The future of America holds opportunities far greater than any, the world has ever known. Ours is destined to become the industrial center of the world. The development of the steel industry will give birth to scores of other related industries. Furniture and household equipment will be made of steel, and it will serve in the place of lumber in a thousand other ways. It will give us skyscrapers taller than anything man has ever constructed in the entire history of the world. It will supplant lumber in the building of houses. It will span the widest rivers with bridges that are safe and indestructible. It will enable us to supplant the horse and buggy with speedy automobiles; and remember, the automobile industry alone is going to create opportunities for thousands of men of vision.

And do not forget that all this advancement of the American way of life will take place through the Master Mind alliance of the men who are the leaders of American industry and American finance. Billions of dollars of organized capital will be required. The money will come from the savings of the American people, and it can be truthfully said that the great Master Mind of America will, therefore, be a composite mind consisting of the individual assets of the minds and the money of millions of people. This is Democracy in its purest form! Such a democracy is one in which the brains, the spirit, and the finances of the people will be coordinated and used for the development of American opportunity in a thousand different directions.

Let this truth become the common property of all the people of America and we will hear less complaint against the "capitalists of Wall Street" and the "predatory interests." The real capitalists of America are the people whose savings are invested in the great industrial enterprises.

Definiteness of Purpose, if backed by the will to win, is a road map to success.

Hill: Your description of the sources of American Opportunity is both dramatic and thrilling, Mr. Carnegie. I have never previously heard Americanism analyzed in terms of its Five Foundation Stones, nor had I ever understood these fundamentals to be the real source of all American Opportunity. But I see that they are. Will you now go back to the analysis of the Master Mind principle as it applies to the individual efforts of the American people? Describe, if you will, the various uses an individual may make of this great principle, in his daily endeavour to appropriate his portion of American Opportunity.

Carnegie: I was coming back to that, as a climax for this chapter on the Master Mind. But, as I have stated, it is essential for an individual to know where we get our right to speak of this country as the richest and the freest country in the world, before he can appropriate and use his portion of this freedom and riches. The privileges available to the American people, like all other rights and privileges, have back of them a source of power. Privileges do not spring, mushroom-like, from the earth. They must be created and maintained! The founders of our American form of government, through their foresight and wisdom, laid the foundation for all American freedom and riches. But they only laid the foundation. It is the responsibility and the duty of every person who claims any portion of this freedom and riches, to contribute his share in the maintenance of these privileges.

I have already described the most important relationship in which an individual can make use of the Master Mind principle: the relationship of marriage. I will now analyze some of the other individual uses of this great universal principle, as it may be applied in the development of various human relationships contributory to the attainment of one's Major Purpose in life. I want every reader to recognize the fact that the attainment of his Major Purpose (his highest aim in life) can be reached only by a series of steps, and that every thought he thinks, every transaction in which he engages in his relationship with others, every plan he creates, and every mistake he makes, has a vital bearing on his ability to attain his chosen goal. The mere choice of a Definite Major Purpose in life, even though it be written out and fully fixed in one's mind, will not ensure the successful realization of that purpose. One's Major Purpose must be backed up and followed through by continuous effort, the most important part of which consists of the sort of effort that is applied in relationship with other people. With this truth well fixed in the mind it is not difficult to understand how necessary it is for an individual to be careful in his choice of associates, especially those with whom he comes into close daily contact.

Here, then, are some of the sources of human relationship which the man with a Definite Major Purpose in life must cultivate, organize, and use in his progress toward his chosen goal.

Occupational – Outside of the relationship of marriage there is no other form of relationship as important as that which exists between a man and those with whom he works, in the pursuit of his daily occupation. There is a tendency, and it is one that is common to all men, for an individual to take on the mannerism, the mental attitude, the philosophy of life, the political viewpoint, the economic leaning, and the other general traits of the most outspoken of the men with whom he associates in his daily work. The tragedy of this tendency is the fact that not always is the most outspoken man among one's daily associates the soundest thinker; and very often he is a man with the poorest character!

Also, the most outspoken man usually is an individual who has no Definite Major Purpose of his own; therefore, he devotes his time and his efforts to endeavouring to belittle the man who has such a purpose. Men with sound character, who know exactly what they want from life, usually have the wisdom to keep their own counsel, and seldom if ever do they waste any of their time trying to discourage other men. They are so busily engaged in promoting their own purpose that they have no time to waste with anything or anyone that does not contribute, in one way or another, to their benefit.

Realizing that one may find in almost every group with which a man comes into contact in his daily work, some persons whose influence and cooperation may be helpful, the discriminating man with a Definite Major Purpose in life will prove his wisdom if he forms close friendships only with those who can be, and are willing to be, mutually beneficial to him. The others he will tactfully avoid! Naturally, he will seek his closest alliances with men whom he recognizes to possess traits of character and knowledge and experience greater than his own, and of course he will not overlook those holding positions higher in rank than his own, with his eye on the day when he can excel them! Remembering the words of Abraham Lincoln, who said, "I will study and prepare myself, and some day my chance will come."

The man with a constructive Definite Major Purpose in life will never envy his superiors: he will study their methods and appropriate their knowledge instead. You may put it down as a sound prophecy that the man who spends his time finding fault with his Boss will never be a successful Boss on his own account.

The greatest soldiers are those who can take and carry out the orders of their superiors in rank. Those who cannot or will not do this never will become successful leaders in military operations. The same is true of the man in a private job. If he fails to emulate the man above him, in a spirit of harmony, he will never benefit greatly from his association with that man. No fewer than twenty men have risen from the ranks of labour, in my organization, and have made themselves richer than they needed to be. They did not get thereby finding fault with me, although they well knew that I have many faults; but they promoted themselves by appropriating and using the experience of everyone with whom they came into daily contact, including myself.

The man with a Definite Major Purpose will take careful inventory of every person with whom he is associated in his daily work, and he will look upon every such person as a possible source of knowledge or influence that he can borrow and use in his own promotion. If he looks around him intelligently he will discover that his daily place of labour is literally a school room in which he can acquire the greatest of all educations, that which comes from experience.

"How can one make the greatest use of this sort of schooling?" Some will ask. No one ever does anything without a motive. Men lend their experience and their knowledge and their aid to other men because they have been given a sufficient motive for doing so. The man who relates himself to his daily associates in a friendly, cooperative mental attitude stands a better chance of learning from them than the man who is belligerent, irritable, discourteous or neglectful in the little amenities of courtesy that exist between all cultured people. The old saying that a man can catch more flies with honey than he can with salt might well be remembered by the man who wishes to learn from his daily associates who know more than he does, and whose cooperation he needs and seeks.

Educational – No man's education ever is finished. The man whose Definite Major Purpose in life is of noteworthy proportions must continue to be a student, and he must learn from every possible source—especially those sources from which he can gather specialized knowledge and experience related to his major purpose.

The public libraries are free. They offer a great array of organized knowledge on every subject known to civilization. They carry, in every language, the sum total of all of man's knowledge. The successful man makes it his business to read books, and to learn important facts concerning his chosen work which have come from the experience of other men who have gone before him. It has been said that a man cannot consider himself even an elementary student of any subject until he has availed himself, as far as possible, of all knowledge on that subject that has been preserved for him through the experience of others.

A man's reading program should be as carefully chosen as his daily diet, for it, too, is food without which he cannot grow mentally. The man who spends all his reading time on the funny papers and the sex magazines is not headed toward great achievement; you may put that down as definite and accurate. The same may be said of the man who does not include in his daily reading program some form of reading which definitely provides him with knowledge which he can use in one way or another in the attainment of his major purpose. Random reading may be pleasing, but it seldom is helpful in connection with a man's occupation.

Reading, however, is not the only source of education available to a man. By a careful choice among his daily associates in his work, and his social relationships, a man may ally himself with men from whom he can acquire a very liberal education, through ordinary conversation. Business and professional clubs offer an opportunity for one to form alliances of great educational benefit, provided a man chooses his clubs and his individual associations in those clubs, with a definite objective in mind. Through this sort of association many men have formed both business and social acquaintances of great value to them in carrying out the object of their major purpose.

No man can go through life successfully without the habit of cultivating friends. The word "contact," as it is used in connection with personal acquaintanceship, is an important word. If a man makes it a part of his duty to extend his list of personal "contacts," he will find the habit of use to him in ways that cannot be foreseen while he is cultivating his acquaintances, but the time will come when they will be ready and willing to aid him if he has done a good job of selling himself to them.

Church Activity – No philosophy of individual achievement would be complete without at least a brief reference to the benefits of a church alliance. It is not my intention to advocate any particular religion, as I believe a man's religion is something that is so intimate and definitely a part of himself that he should be left alone to form his own ideas of religion. But it does come within the scope of my privileges, as an analyst of the causes of success and failure, to call attention to the many benefits a man may gain from a church alliance; and I have reference to purely economic advantages, as well as to spiritual benefits available through a church relationship.

The church is among the most desirable of sources through which to meet and cultivate people, because it brings people together at a time and under circumstances which inspire the spirit of fellowship among men. Every man needs some source through which he can associate with his neighbours under circumstances which will enable him to exchange thoughts with them for the sake of mutual understanding and friendship, quite aside from all thoughts connected with pecuniary gain. The man who shuts himself up in his own shell, and engages in but little or no outside form of intercourse with his neighbours, soon becomes selfish and narrow in his views.

Aside from this viewpoint, the habit of church attendance enables a man to form acquaintances with people who may, and often do, become of great help to him in the promotion of his business, or the sale of his personal services. People who attend church together soon establish between themselves a bond of mutual confidence which may serve them in both business and social relationships outside of the church.

Political Alliance – It is both the duty and the privilege of every American citizen to interest himself in politics and exercise his right to help, through the ballot, to place worthy men and women in public office. The political party to which a man belongs, if any, is of much less importance than the question of his exercising his privilege of voting. If politics becomes smeared with dishonest practices, there is no one to blame but the people who have it in their power to keep dishonest, unworthy, and inefficient people out of office. In addition to the privilege of voting and the duty it carries with it, one should not overlook the benefits to be gained from an active interest in politics, through "contacts" and alliances with people who may become helpful in the attainment of one's major purpose.

In some occupations, political influence becomes a definite and important factor in the promotion of one's personal interests. Business and professional people certainly should not neglect the possibility of promoting their interests through active political alliances. While one may not care to become a politician, or become a candidate for public office, the possibilities in connection with the obligations to voters that public office-holders incur may be converted into an asset of great benefit to every voter, in the promotion of his own private occupation. The alert individual, who understands the necessity of reaching out in every possible direction for friendly allies he can use in achieving the object of his major purpose in life, will make the fullest use of his privilege of voting.

Social Alliances – Here is an almost unlimited, fertile field for the cultivation of friendly "contacts." It is particularly available to the married man whose wife understands the art of making friends through social activities. Such a wife can convert her home and her social activities into a priceless asset for her husband, if his occupation is one that requires him to make friends with people on a sizable scale.

Most professional men, whose professional ethics forbid direct advertising or self-promotion, may make telling use of their social privileges—especially if they have wives with a bent for social activities. One successful life insurance agent sells more than a million dollars' worth of insurance every year, with the aid of his wife who is a member of a prominent Business Woman's Club. His wife's part is simple. She entertains her fellow club members in her home, along with their husbands, where her husband becomes acquainted with them under friendly circumstances.

A lawyer's wife is credited with helping him build the most lucrative law practice in a Middle Western city, by the simple process of entertaining, through her social activities, the wives of wealthy businessmen. The possibilities in this direction are endless.

One of the major advantages of friendly alliances with people in a variety of walks of life is the opportunity such contacts provide for "round table" discussions. If one's acquaintances are sufficiently numerous and varied, they may become a valuable source of information on a wide range of subjects, thus leading to a form of intercourse which is essential for the development of versatility of thought.

I have observed, on many occasions, when groups of men get together and enter into round table discussions on any subject, that this sort of free and spontaneous expression of thought enriches the minds of all who participate in it. Every man needs to reinforce his own ideas and plans with new food for thought which he can acquire only through frank and honest discussion with people whose ideas differ from his own.

The preacher who preaches the same sermon over and over again, without injecting into it new ideas appropriated from the thoughts of other men, will soon find himself preaching to empty pews. The writer who becomes a top-notcher and remains in that exalted position must add continuously to his own stock of knowledge by appropriating the thoughts and the ideas of others, through personal contacts and by reading.

A mind that remains brilliant, alert, receptive, and flexible must be fed continuously from the storehouse of other minds. If this renewal is neglected the mind atrophies, the same as an arm that is taken out of use. This is in accordance with nature's laws. Study nature's plan and you will discover that every living thing, from the smallest insect to the complicated machinery of a human being, grows and remains healthy only through constant use. Only dead objects wear from use. Round-table discussions not only add to one's store of usable knowledge, but they develop and expand the power of the mind.

The person who stops studying the day he finishes school will never become an educated person, no matter how much knowledge he may have accumulated while he was going to school. Life itself is a great school and everything that inspires thought is a teacher. The wiseman knows this; moreover, he makes it a part of his daily routine to contact other minds with the object of developing his own mind through exchange of thoughts.

We see, therefore, that the Master Mind principle has an unlimited scope of practical use. It is the medium by which an individual may supplement the power of his own mind with the knowledge and the experience and the mental attitude of other minds. As one man aptly expressed the idea: "If I give you one of my dollars in return for one of your dollars, each of us has no more than he had to start with; but if I give you a thought in return for one of your thoughts, each of us has gained a hundred per cent dividend on our investment." No form of human relationship is as profitable as that through which men exchange thoughts, and it is surprising but true that one may pick up from the mind of the humblest person an idea of the first magnitude.

Let me illustrate what I mean through the story of a preacher who picked from the mind of the janitor of his church an idea that led to the attainment of his major purpose in life. The preacher's name was Russell Conwell, and his major purpose was the founding of a college he had long desired to establish. The fly in the ointment was lack of the necessary money, a tidy sum of more than a million dollars.

One day the Reverend Russell Conwell stopped to chat with the janitor who was busily at work, cutting the grass on the church lawn. The janitor had a philosophical trend of the mind. As they stood there, talking of the odds and ends of light conversation, Conwell casually remarked that the grass on the lawn adjoining the church yard was much greener and better kept than that on their own yard. He intended his remark, of course, as a mild reprimand to the old caretaker.

With a broad grin on his face, the man said, "The grass looks green on the other side of the fence because we are used to the grass on this side." That remark planted in the fertile mind of Russell Conwell the seed of an idea—just a bare tiny seed, mind you—which led to the solution of his major purpose in life. From that humble remark was born an idea for a lecture which Conwell composed, and delivered more than four thousand times. He called it "Acres of Diamonds." The central idea of the lecture was this: A man need not seek his opportunity in the distance, but he can find it right where he stands, by recognizing the fact that the grass on the other side of the fence is not greener than it is where one stands: it only appears to be so.

The lecture yielded an income, during the life of Russell Conwell, of more than four million dollars. It was published in book form and became a best-seller throughout the country for many years after he passed on. The money was used to found and maintain Temple University, one of the great schools of America. The idea around which the lecture was built did more than found a university. It enriched the minds of thousands of people, by influencing them to look for opportunity right where they stood. The philosophy of the lecture is as sound today as it was the day it came from the mind of a philosophical yard worker.

Remember this: Every active brain is a potential source of inspiration from which one may procure an idea, or the mere seed of an idea, of priceless value in the solution of one's personal problems. Sometimes great ideas spring from humble minds, but generally they come from the minds of those closest to one, where the Master Mind relationship has been deliberately established and maintained. The most profitable idea of my own career came to me one afternoon when Charlie Schwab and I were on the golf course. As we finished our shots on the thirteenth hole, Charlie looked up at me with a sheepish grin on his face, and said, "I'm three points up on you at this hole, Chief; but I have just thought of an idea that should give you a lot of time to play golf."

My curiosity prompted me to inquire into the nature of his idea. He gave it to me, in one brief sentence, every word of which was worth, roughly speaking, a million dollars. "Consolidate all your plants into one big corporation," he exclaimed, "and sell out to Wall Street." Nothing more was said about the matter during the game, but that evening I began to turn the suggestion over in my mind and think about it. Before I went to sleep I had converted the seed of his idea into a definite plan. The following week I sent Charlie Schwab to New York to deliver a speech before a group of Wall Street bankers, among them J. Pierpont Morgan. The substance of the speech was a plan for the organization of the United States Steel Corporation, through which

I consolidated all my steel interests and retired from active business, with more money than any one person needs. Now, let me emphasize one point. Charlie Schwab's idea might never have been born, and I probably never would have received the benefit of it, if I had not made it my business to encourage the creation of ideas. This encouragement was provided through a close and continuous Master Mind relationship with the members of my Master Mind group, among them Schwab.

"Contact," let me repeat, is an important word! It is much more important if we add to it the word "harmonious!" Through harmonious relationships with the minds of other men, an individual may have the full use of his capacity to create ideas. The man who overlooks this great truth thereby condemns himself eternally to mediocrity. No man is smart enough to project his influence very far into the world without the friendly cooperation of other people. Drive this thought home in every way you can, in your presentation of the Philosophy of American Achievement, for it is sufficient unto itself to open the road of success to thousands of men and women who might otherwise go through life without coming within sight of their major purpose in life, let alone the attainment of that purpose.

Too many people look for success in the distance, afar from where they are; and altogether too often they search for it through complicated plans based upon a belief in "miracles" and luck. As Russell Conwell so aptly stated the matter in his famous lecture, some people seem to think the grass is greener on the other side of the fence from where they stand, and they pass up the "Acres of Diamonds" in the form of ideas and opportunities available to them through the minds of their daily associates.

I found my "Acres of Diamonds" right where I stood, while looking into the glow of a blast furnace that was so hot I could penetrate it only with my thoughts. I remember well the first day I began to sell myself the idea of becoming the leader of a great steel industry instead of remaining an unimportant puddler in another man's "Acre of Diamonds."

At first the thought was not very definite; it was more a wish than a definite purpose. Soon I began bringing it back into my mind and encouraging it to take up its regular residence there, until came the day, finally, when the idea began to drive me instead of my driving it.

That day I began with earnestness to work my "diamond mine," and it was surprising to learn how quickly a definite purpose finds a way of translating itself into its physical equivalent. The main thing is to know what one wants. The next thing of greatest importance is to begin digging for diamonds right where one stands, using whatever tools may be at hand, even if they be nothing but the tools of thought. In proportion to the faithful use of tools at hand will one receive other and better tools. The man who understands the Master Mind principle and makes use of it, will find the necessary tools much more quickly than the fellow who knows nothing of this principle.

No doubt it will be interesting for some of the readers to learn how and where I first acquired an understanding of the Master Mind principle to which I owe, more than to all else, the financial success with which my work has been rewarded.

Well, I'll tell you the story and in doing so, you will have a better understanding of my reason for including church attendance as one of the important sources for profitable use of the Master Mind principle. Of course all who know me know that I have never emphasized my religious views, or my church attendance, in the sense of holding myself out as an example to be emulated; but I have made it a part of my regular life program to lay aside all thoughts of material things, at least one day out of every seven, by reading a book or listening to a lecture or a sermon.

One Sunday morning, I heard a clergyman preach a sermon in which he gave a vivid description of what he believed Christ would do if He lived in a world where business and industry were the dominating interests of the people. In a very dramatic manner, he drew a picture of Christ and His Twelve Disciples, living in our modern world, transformed into modern-day life, and described them seated around a table as a board of directors of a great industry. He placed modern words in the mouths of Christ and the Disciples and painted an impressive picture of how he believed they would manage a business, if they lived and moved in an industrial age such as ours.

I was only a young, unknown labourer, but that sermon planted in my mind the seed of the Master Mind principle. I began to think about it. I began to talk about it with my fellow labourers, and very soon two of my closest associates began to catch a vision of its stupendous possibilities. We clothed the idea with our practical understanding of the steel industry. Very soon, almost before we fully realized the power of the principle we had stumbled upon, we had crystalized our conversation into a Definite Major Purpose which led to the source from which we procured the necessary working capital for my first industrial venture.

This is a world of cynicism and doubt and you will find plenty of men who will tell you that they do not attend church because preachers talk only of a world of which they know not; that their ideas are impractical and unsuited for use in a work-a-day world where a man must attend to the needs of his stomach before he can do much about the salvation of his soul. No wise man will be misled by this sort of philosophy. The church is a place where one may find fuel for the fire of thought. It may be true that preachers sometimes talk too much about a future life and too little about the life we are living in this world. The fact remains, nevertheless, that I found the way out of poverty into riches through an idea planted in my mind by a preacher in a church.

Do not misunderstand me to say that the church is the only place where one may become inspired with sound ideas that help in the solution of material problems; nor do I intend to convey the impression that the church is always the best place for such inspiration. I do wish to emphasize the fact, however, that friendly human intercourse through the operation of the Master Mind principle, whatever may be its source, is essential for mind development and growth, and the church often offers a favourable environment for the development of this principle.

Every mind needs contact with other minds for the food of expansion and growth. The discriminating person chooses, with the greatest of care, the types of minds with which he associates most intimately, recognizing that he takes on a definite part of the personality of every person with whom he associates regularly. I wouldn't give a fig for a man who does not make it his business to seek the company of people who know more and have more influence than he himself has, for it is true that as day follows night, so a man rises to the level of his superiors or falls to the level of his inferiors, according to which class he emulates through his choice of close associates.

It is a well-known fact that I surrounded myself with a Master Mind group of men who knew more than I about the making and the marketing of steel. If I had not done so I would never have been recognized as the leading manufacturer of steel.

Hill: I follow your explanation clearly enough, Mr. Carnegie, but there is one thing you have not explained and it is bothering me quite definitely. What I would like to know is the rule by which one is governed in choosing, as his Master Mind allies, men who have superior ability and knowledge. It occurs to me that men of superior ability will not be easily influenced to ally themselves with a man of inferior ability. How may one overcome this obstacle in the building of a Master Mind alliance?

Carnegie: I am very glad you asked that question, for it gives me an opportunity to set you right on this point. Let us begin by calling attention to the nine basic motives which serve as the moving spirit in all that people do or refrain from doing. Men go into alliance with other men because of some benefits they expect to get from the alliance.

The man who controls his own mind may control practically everything else he desires.

It often happens that a man with very little ability in connection with many subjects, has experience and knowledge of great practical value along some one particular line. If he can show that his ideas are sound that they can be made to yield profits, he will have no difficulty in inducing others to join forces with him in the promotion and development of his ideas, although his associates may be his superiors in many respects outside of his own specialized knowledge.

Take my own case, for example: I was only a common labourer, but I conceived certain ideas in connection with the making and marketing of steel which were in advance of the accustomed methods in use in that industry. The novelty of my ideas, plus my ability to sell them to others, gave me the dominating position in an alliance with men who willingly supplied the necessary working capital to develop the ideas.

In most respects, these men were my superiors. In the making of steel, under my plan, I was their superior, and they acknowledged me as such. Their specialty was the manipulation and use of capital for a profit. My specialty was making steel by improved methods. We needed each other. The men who supplied the capital could not make steel, but I could show them how to make it more economically than it had ever been made before. With the necessary working capital at my disposal, it was a simple matter for me to surround myself with men who had the technical ability needed in the making of steel. They were motivated, in their alliance with me, by their desire for financial gain. They needed me as badly as I needed them, because their specialties did not include the promotional ability necessary to convert their talents into money. Since I possessed that ability, they willingly joined forces with me.

I'll give you another typical example of how men with practical ideas induce men with superior ability to join them, through the Master Mind principle. In the city of Detroit, there is a man by the name of Henry Ford. He had but little schooling and his personality is nothing of which to boast, but he created an idea that attracted to him the technical ability and the working capital necessary to give his idea great commercial value.

His idea, as everyone knows, is a self-propelled vehicle of transportation known as an automobile. He devoted a lot of time and thought to his idea, and experimented with it until he proved it was of commercial value. His next step was to induce one of his acquaintances to provide a small amount of working capital with which to begin manufacturing his automobile. With the aid of his newly formed ally he induced the Dodge brothers and other men with technical and mechanical ability to become a part of his Master Mind alliance. Perhaps his allies had more ability, in many respects, than Henry Ford had; but the idea was his and they accorded him the privilege of becoming the dominating factor in the alliance.

This is the usual method of procedure through which men surround themselves with allies who have greater ability than they themselves possess. Always there is a motive back of such alliances. The most common motive is that of a desire for financial gain. I want you to watch this man Ford, because he will one day dominate the automobile industry of America. Watch him very closely, for he is a philosopher as well as a man with a sound mechanical idea, and you may see how a man can begin at scratch here in America, with nothing to go on but a sound idea and climb to great heights of achievement.

While we are on the subject of ideas I wish to call attention to the fact that ideas rule the world! They are the seeds from which all human achievements germinate. A man who can create a sound idea can always find both the brains and the ability, as well as the necessary capital, for its development and promotion.

Speaking of capital, it should be remembered that money, without the ability of men who are skilled in its use, is of little value in any business. The real capital back of any business consists of both the physical assets measurable in terms of money, and the brains necessary in the management of those assets, with strong emphasis on the latter.

Get this picture of the nature of capital well fixed in mind and you will have a better understanding of the procedure by which men with sound ideas manage to surround themselves with men who are their superiors, in many ways, for the profitable promotion of their ideas. An idea, no matter how sound, may be and it generally is worth but little or nothing until it is backed with money and commercially exploited. Very seldom does one man have the ability to create commercially sound ideas and possess, also, the necessary money with which to promote his ideas. Here is the factual circumstance which makes it comparatively easy for a man with a sound commercial idea to ally himself with a Master Mind group made up of men of superior ability but lacking the creative ability to originate sound ideas.

Sometimes the man with a sound idea has considerable difficulty in convincing men with money of the commercial possibilities of his idea; especially he is likely to meet indifference and opposition if the idea be basically new and untried. A recent example of this nature will serve to illustrate what I mean. The Wright brothers created a very sound, but new and untried idea, when they made a machine that would fly. The world had never seen a machine that could be flown through the air with a man at the controls. Without a precedent to follow, the Wrights built such a machine and they proved to their own satisfaction that it was practical.

At first the newspaper men were so skeptical that they would not take the time to investigate this flying machine. They believed that a flying machine was not practical because they had never seen such a machine and they had never heard of one. If the Wright brothers had been just average men, they would have become discouraged and would have given up their idea before it was accepted by the world. But they are not average men; they have potential successes. They have a Definite Major Purpose and the courage to stand by their purpose until they achieve its object. With the aid of the Master Mind principle they will attract to men with the necessary capital and other men with the necessary technical ability to perfect and promote their idea until they force the world to accept it. The flying machine industry is in the offing, but the time will come and very soon at that, when travcl by air will be as common as travel by train or automobile at the present.

This is the way of all human progress and it has been so from the dawn of civilization to this very day. Men accept new ideas slowly and unwillingly! To be forewarned is to be forearmed; therefore, be sure to caution the students of the philosophy of Achievement against the common habit of quitting the moment, the going becomes difficult.

Thomas A. Edison had hard going at first. Well do I remember how the world hooted and howled its contempt for Edison when he first announced that he had perfected a practical incandescent lamp that could be lighted with electricity. Edison went through the same experience that every man with a new or an improved idea goes through but Edison was a man with a definite purpose and he stood by his purpose through more than ten thousand failures and disappointments, to see, at last, the triumph of courage over fear and doubt.

Hill: I am glad to have your counsel on the subject of persistence, Mr. Carnegie, for I shall probably need to follow it for a long time before I get the world to accept a new philosophy of individual achievement.

Carnegie: Yes, you will need a lot of persistence—more than is required in most undertakings, because you will need persistence to carry you through the long years of work you will have to do before you organize the philosophy and you will need it before you get the world to accept the results of your labour. That is why I am stressing the importance of your taking notice of the experience of the men before you who, without a single exception, met with skepticism and doubt before they got their ideas accepted.

Your success or failure will hinge largely, if not entirely, upon your capacity to carry on without the approval of the world, until your work gains recognition. Nevertheless, you do have a combination of motives to supply you with the courage and the moving spirit to keep on until you get to where you have started.

In the first place, your gift to the world of its first practical philosophy of individual achievement will bring you more fame and public recognition than any man needs to satisfy his thirst for recognition.

In the second place, your triumph will bring you more financial reward than you will need.

In the third place, the service you will render the world, through your work, will bring you happiness of an enduring nature, of a quality and a quantity that you could find in no other way. Keep these thoughts in mind when discouragement overtakes you and they will help you to remove every obstacle that gets in your way.

If you do your work well, you will live to see the day when you will have projected your influence into every part of the civilized world. Your name will become a byword in every village, town, and city in America. Your works will be translated into every language and your contribution to the world will have been of a more practical and enduring nature than that of all the teachers of abstract philosophy known to civilization, from Plato and his school of thought, on down to Emerson and the recent philosophers. Get this viewpoint and hold fast to it, but don't let it get you! If you ever reach the point at which you begin to take yourself too seriously or feel that you are indispensable to the world, you will have outlived your usefulness. Approach your job with humility of the heart, keeping ever in the uppermost part of your mind the thought that you are only a student searching the lives of men for knowledge about life and about living that will be helpful to those who have neither the ability nor the inclination to spend twenty or thirty years looking for the principles of human achievement.

You will become great only in proportion to the help which you extend to others in finding themselves, but never by feeling your own greatness!

Before I pass on I will open many doors to you and give you free access to the minds of many men of distinguished achievement. If you impress these men as one who takes himself or his work too seriously, or lead them to believe from your slightest deed or word that you are working only for your own personal aggrandizement, they will close up on you like clams and you'll get no co-operation from them. Approach them with sincerity of purpose written in your face and on your heart, and they will drop their own work and give you the full benefit of the richness of their own lives.

I will send you to Dr. Alexander Graham Bell, the inventor of the long-distance telephone and Dr. Elmer R. Gates, the great American scientist who has spent his life in research in connection with the operation of the human mind and I will send you to no fewer than a score of other distinguished men whose entire life-work will become an open book for you to appropriate and use, but you will get nothing from any of these men unless you approach them with evidence that you are labouring to give the world a better philosophy of individual achievement than any it has at present.

Remember, a man can get almost anything he asks for, within reason, if he seeks it on behalf of the yet unborn and the world at large; but let him show by his acts and words that he is seeking co-operation for purely personal benefits and he will find the world cold and indifferent. If I seem to emphasize this truth to the point of personal effrontery, I do so because you and every person embarking on a task such as the one you have undertaken needs to understand this trait of mankind. I give it to you, not only for your own guidance, but I ask that you pass it on, through the Philosophy of Achievement, to others who also need it.

If you wish a practical illustration of what happens when this principle is put into operation by a man who proves to the community that he is working for the interests of the people and not for his own self-promotion alone, study the experience of the candidate for public office who rises up with righteous indignation because of the political evils of his day and goes before the people as a reform candidate, promising them that he will sacrifice his own personal interests and his time for their welfare. I have known of more than one instance in which such men were swept into office by overwhelming majorities.

Just a little while ago a certain district in a large American city became so badly abused through the sins of a mayor who had allied himself with the underworld, that it was unsafe for young people to enter that section of the city. The politicians were appealed to in vain. Finally, a clergyman made up his mind to do something about it. Despite his lack of experience in the ways of politics he selected a well-known businessman as his choice for mayor and went into the offending district with his coat off and his fighting blood boiling to a white heat, and told the people in no uncertain terms that he was going to stay there until they helped him put a decent man in office. Night after night he stumped the district, speaking from a platform he had mounted on a wagon, winding up his speech each time with these words: "I am asking your cooperation, not for any benefit to myself, but for the sake of your children and your neighbor's children who are entitled to an example of decency on the part of all you older people."

His candidate was swept into office with the biggest majority that city ever gave any mayor! So the story goes, in all human relationships. The whole world wants to help the man who forgets himself and gives his services for the benefit of others. If I am not mistaken, this was the idea of a lowly carpenter who, nearly two thousand years ago, gave His services and His life for the betterment of others. His influence has spread until it is now the greatest single influence for good that the world has ever known and His philosophy is as sound today as it was when He preached it.

There are three sides to all disputes: your side, the other fellow's side, and the right side.

I do not wish to make a preacher of you, but I do wish to bring to your attention a simple rule of human relationship that was given to the world by the greatest philosopher of all times and I sincerely hope you will not neglect to pass on to the world the suggestion I have given you of His philosophy. If the time ever comes in this country or in any other, when people become so cold and ultrapractical that they look with contempt upon the philosophy of the Nazarene, the world will be in a bad way indeed. Besides, I want you to remember that it was this same humble carpenter who gave the world its first demonstration of the soundness of the Master Mind principle. Some theologies may have drifted far afield from the original teachings of the Nazarene and the business world may, therefore, sometimes have just reasons for looking upon modern applications of religion as being impractical in the management of industry, but let the world remember that the theology of some fallible interpreter and the simple teachings of the Master are two separate and distinct things. I have never held myself out as a model follower of any one modern interpretation of religion, but I do know what the Master said about human relationships and I do know, from practical experience and observation of the methods of businessmen, good and bad, that His philosophy is as sound and applicable today as it was when He taught it.

Analysis of chapter two the master mind principle

by Napoleon Hill

As Mr. Carnegie has so convincingly stated, the Master Mind principle is a practical medium through which one may appropriate and use the education, intelligence, and personal experience of other people; therefore, it is the medium with which one may overcome practically every obstacle that has to be dealt with in the attainment of the object of one's major purpose.

Through the aid of the Master Mind principle, one may examine the stars of the heavens without being an astronomer.

With the aid of this principle one may see and understand the structure of this earth on which we live, without being a geologist.

One may watch Nature as she produces a butterfly from a grub worm, without being a biologist.

Through this principle one may know the nature and the use of drugs and chemicals without being a chemist.

One may know about the history of mankind without having lived through it.

All these possibilities, and more, are available to the person who understands how to apply this universal principle, therefore, it takes a position of the first magnitude in the philosophy of individual achievement.

No liberties have been taken with the foregoing recitation of Mr. Carnegie's interpretation of the Master Mind principle and its role in the philosophy of achievement. At his request the philosophy has been presented, as nearly as possible, in his exact words.

The following are my additional observations about the Master Mind principle.

Suggestions for beginners in the use of the master mind principle

Here is an outline of the directions for the practical use of the Master Mind principle which I give to all beginners:

(a) For all practical purposes, the student may assume that there are two types of Master Mind alliances. First, the purely personal type, consisting of relatives, close personal friends, religious advisers, and social acquaintances with whom one may become allied for social enjoyment or educational purposes, without any intention of converting the alliance into material or financial gain. Second, occupational, business or professional alliances, consisting of those chosen entirely for financial, economic or professional advancement for profit. Harmony is the watchword for success in both of these groups. Remember that in both groups one of the major considerations which one must give to one's allies in return for their sympathy, loyalty, knowledge, experience, creative ability, harmony and cooperation is a return, in full measure, of these same qualities.

(b) Select, as members of your Master Mind alliance, in both groups, men and women who are best suited to your needs. Choose those who are most likely to remain in complete sympathy with your Definite Major Purpose. Keep the object of your major purpose closely confined to your own mind and to the minds of those you have chosen to aid you in achieving that purpose. If you find you have chosen any unsuitable member of your alliance, dismiss the unwise choice and make a new selection.

(c) Six or seven people usually constitute the most favourable number for harmonious cooperation. A larger number sometimes becomes unwieldy. For purely social alliances (exclusive of business undertakings where technical ability is essential) a smaller number will suffice, the number depending, of course, upon the nature and purpose of the alliance.

(d) Members of a Master Mind alliance should remain, at all times, in close communication with one another. They should have a regular meeting time just as the Board of Directors of a well-managed business meets at regular periods. It is not essential, however, for all members to be present at every meeting.

(e) At formal meetings of a Master Mind group, ways and means for the attainment of the object of one's Definite Major Purpose or the attainment of any minor object leading toward the achievement of one's major purpose, should be thoroughly analysed through a discussion in which all members participate, so that final plans will represent the combined experience, knowledge, ingenuity, strategy, and imagination of all the individuals in the alliance. However, the actual act of carrying out any plan created by the group is the sole responsibility of the leader. Do not expect others to tell you what to do, when to do it, where to do it, and how to do it and then go ahead and do it for you!

(f) Remember, always, that a burning desire, definitely stated, backed by faith, is the beginning of all achievement, and the very core around which the Master Mind principle operates successfully. Desire—deeply seated, definitely defined desire—is the starting point from which the Master Mind can be applied. There is nothing available to an individual through his own efforts except that which is obtainable through definite desire. Therefore, let the object of your major purpose in life become an obsessional desire!

(g) Remember, also, that one's mental attitude is a contagious form of energy which extends to and influences every member of one's Master Mind group; therefore, go into your Master Mind sessions in a spirit of self-reliance based upon absolute faith in the attainment of the object of your major purpose. There can be no compromise with one's self concerning this state of mind called faith. It is the unseen power that unites the minds of a Master Mind group into one mind, once it becomes the dominating factor of each individual mind of the group. Faith and fear are the two opposite ends of the pole of energy created by a Master Mind alliance, one representing the positive end of the pole, the other representing the negative end.

Faith permits one to approach within communicating distance of God. Fear holds one at arm's length and makes communication impossible.

Faith evolves a great leader whose vision knows no bounds; Fear creates a cringing follower.

Faith makes men courageous and honourable at trade; Fear makes men dishonest, undependable, and stealthy-minded.

Faith causes one to look for and to expect to find the best there is in man; Fear discovers only man's short comings and deficiencies.

Faith unmistakably identifies itself through the look in one's eyes, in the expression on one's face, in the tone of one's voice and in one's every act. Fear identifies itself through the same avenues, where all who will, may recognize its presence.

Faith attracts people in a spirit of willingness to co-operate; Fear repels people and causes them to become uncommunicative and unresponsive to one's overtures.

Faith attracts only that which is constructive and creative; Fear attracts only that which is destructive. Test this principle wherever you will, and be convinced of its soundness.

Right works through Faith; Wrong works through Fear. Pitted, one against the other, the man with abundant Faith will win over the man who is motivated by Fear, ninety-nine times out of every hundred; and this because Fear causes a man to plunge ahead without plan or purpose, while Faith moves only on well-defined plans, toward definite ends.

Both Faith and Fear begin, at once, to clothe their objectives in physical realities through the most practical and natural media available.

Faith constructs; Fear tears down. This order never is reversed. Faith can construct an Empire State Building, build a Panama Canal, or give security to a nation. Fear negates all enterprise, both large and small.

Faith and Fear never fraternize. Both cannot and will not occupy the mind at the same time. One or the other must, and always does, dominate.

Fear ushers in the devastating wars and depressions; Faith drives them out again.

Faith can lift the humblest person to heights of great achievement in any calling. Fear can and does make achievement impossible.

Even a horse or a dog knows when its master is afraid, and definitely reflects that Fear in its conduct, thus proving that Fear is contagious.

Faith is a mysterious, irresistible power which the scientists have not been able to isolate or understand. It is Nature's own secret alchemy with which the mind of man is given Spiritual Powers.

Fear will no more mix with Spiritual Power than will oil mix with water.

Faith is a state of mind, and it is every man's privilege to use it. Significant is the fact that the only thing over which any individual has complete control is his state of mind.

When used, Faith removes most of the real and all of the imaginary limitations with which man binds himself in his own mind. No man has ever yet discovered any limitations to the power of Faith.

Faith begins to take possession of the mind when one crystallizes one's hopes, desires, aims and purposes into a burning determination to succeed.

Faith forms a natural affinity with justice; Fear fraternizes with injustice.

Faith is a normal state of mind; Fear is unnatural and abnormal. Whether large or small, to be successful every business must have a leader who can and does inspire Faith in all who serve and are served through that business.

When you no longer have Faith in your aims and hopes, you may as well write "finis" across your record, because you will be through, no matter who you are or what may be your calling.

"For verily I say unto you, if ye have faith as a grain of mustard seed, ye shall say unto this mountain, Remove hence to yonder place, and it shall remove; and nothing shall be impossible unto you."

* * *

I am here stressing an important factor of the Master Mind principle which Mr. Carnegie did not emphasize, namely the state of mind known as Faith. I have done this because experience has proved, times without number, that the habit of friendly discussion of any subject, through what is popularly known as the round-table conference, has a decided tendency to drive away fear and encourage Faith. Most of the men of distinguished achievements have discovered this fact and they have made effective use of it.

It is common knowledge that four distinguished American leaders of industry made use of this principle, over a period of years. Their names are Henry Ford, Thomas A. Edison, Harvey Firestone and John Burroughs, the naturalist. Once a year they laid down their respective business responsibilities and went away together, to some secluded mountain spot, where they entered into a Master Mind alliance for the purpose of exchanging thoughts. When they returned each man of the group brought back all the knowledge he took with him, plus something additional which he acquired from each of the other three. It has been said, by those in a position to know the facts, that every man in the group came back from these yearly pilgrimages with a new and more alert mind.

As Mr. Carnegie has so ably stated, no single mind is complete by itself. All truly great minds have been reinforced through contacts with other minds. Sometimes this reinforcement takes place through sheer chance, without the individual's full knowledge of what is happening or how it is happening, but the truly great minds are the result of deliberate understanding and use of the Master Mind principle. That is why there are but few truly great minds! The Master Mind principle is not a matter of common knowledge to all people, and it was his understanding of this fact that prompted Andrew Carnegie to say that he was presenting to the people of America the better portion of his real riches, by helping to organize all of the principles of success into a philosophy of individual achievement.

Take the successful men wherever you find them and you will observe, if you have the records of their lives available, that their success was due to the application, in one form or another, of the Master Mind principle.

Arthur Brisbane was a newspaper man with no outstanding record of achievement back of him. He formed an alliance with William Randolph Hearst, through which he became Mr. Hearst's confidential adviser. The relationship between the two men brought into operation that silent, unseen power known as Faith, and very soon Mr. Brisbane had lifted himself into a position of prominence, with his name at the head of a column called "Today" on the front page daily of every newspaper owned by Mr. Hearst. Brisbane's popularity grew until his name appeared on the front pages of hundreds of other newspapers throughout the country. His fortune also grew! And so did William Randolph Hearst grow, both in mind power and in material riches. The alliance brought great benefits to both men.

A little while ago Arthur Brisbane died and immediately following his death the great Hearst newspaper empire crumbled and fell to pieces as if it had been built on a foundation of sand. The composite Master Mind that developed the Hearst papers and kept them operating profitably had died with Brisbane. Such circumstances of fact cannot be explained away as being mere coincidences or chance. The understanding mind knows better. Search wherever you will, among the men and women engaged in the more humble pursuits of life, as well as those engaged in the management of empires of business and industry, and you will find the Master Mind principle in evidence wherever an individual is succeeding.

Kate Smith adopted singing as her major purpose in life, but she got off to a bad start. Some people were willing to listen to her sing, but few were willing to pay for the privilege. Through long discouraging months, she sang whenever and wherever she could get an audience, with or without pay. But nothing happened until she formed a Master Mind alliance with an agent, Ted Collins. Then her fortune took a new lease on life. She now sings regularly, on a national radio network and her singing brings her more money for each performance than most singers earn in a whole year, despite the fact that America has a host of unemployed singers, many of whom probably sing better or at least as well as Kate Smith.

Edgar Bergen and "Charlie McCarthy," his irrepressible "stooge," worked up and down Broadway, New York, for many years, for whatever small compensation they could pick up. Most of the time they were gentlemen "at liberty," as theatrical folk say when they are out of employment. Through chance or otherwise, this now nationally famous pair were discovered by Rudy Vallee. Promptly, he introduced them over his radio program to the largest audience to which they had ever played. That was their turning point! The temporary application of the Master Mind principle, operating through the mind of Vallee and Bergen, gave the necessary impetus to a man whom the whole of America now recognizes as a genius in his profession and his stock sailed skyward! He was a genius before the world discovered him, but that was not enough. It never is. A man may make a better mouse-trap than that of his neighbor, but do not be deceived by believing the world will make a beaten path to his door unless and until his superiority is given impetus through the Master Mind principle.

Jack Dempsey was a young, unknown lad who sometimes engaged in boxing matches. He was unskilled in this art and unknown to most of America. Through a stroke of good fortune, he formed a Master Mind alliance with Jack Kearns, and soon thereafter he was on the road to the World's Championship and a fortune. Came a time when the Master Mind arrangement between the two men was broken, and with it went the Dempsey popularity as a fighter and the loss of his technique. The story is too well known among men in the world of sportsmanship to justify a description of the details here. The fact of major importance to be remembered is that when the Master Mind principle is discarded, there goes with it one's chances of permanent success.

The Reverend Frank Crane was an itinerant preacher whose sermons, as he often complained, "hardly yielded enough to keep body and soul together." At the suggestion of a man who understood the Master Mind principle, Frank Crane stopped preaching sermons to small personal congregations and started to write sermonettes to huge unseen audiences through the medium of a newspaper column that appeared in hundreds of newspapers. The man who helped him market his sermonettes, through the application of the Master Mind principle, is authority for the acknowledgment that Crane's annual income, at the time of his death several years back, was well above $75,000, being more in fact than the President of the United States receives.

No matter what may be one's Definite Major Purpose in life, whether it is managing a great industrial empire or preaching sermons, he will achieve outstanding success only by applying the Master Mind. Let this truth sink in and you will be very near the starting point of success such as you, perhaps, have never known before.

The man who sells more life insurance in the State of Ohio than any other life insurance agent was formerly a street car conductor, with little schooling but an insatiable desire to be recognized as a famous man. His method of applying the Master Mind principle in the sale of life insurance is both interesting and educational. While he was still working as a street car conductor, he became a student of the Philosophy of American Achievement. Before he had actually completed his training, he resigned his job with the street car company and went into the business of selling insurance.

Having caught the full spirit and meaning of the Master Mind principle, he began his new occupation by a unique application of this principle. First, he made permanent alliances with several retail stores that sold furniture on the installment plan, through which he arranged for these stores to present a life insurance policy, with the first year's premium fully paid, to every newly married couple who purchased their complete household furnishings from one of these stores.

He then made similar alliances with the sales agents of several different brands of automobiles. Spurred on by his success in these fields, he entered into alliances with several investment firms through which they ensured the lives of all who purchased homes from them. Next, he made similar alliances with three saving banks, through which the banks ensured the lives of all new depositors who maintained a certain minimum balance to their credit. The first year of his operations this young man earned considerably more than the street car company had paid him during the entire ten years he had worked for the company. He now has several other life insurance agents working for him in other parts of the country and his income is said to be much greater than the entire annual earnings of the street car company for which he formerly worked.

A few facts about this man will serve to explain his success. His schooling and his personal appearance were decidedly against him.

He is a small, thin man, who looks as if the thing he needs most is a good square meal. In most respects, he is inferior to the average man, and he knows it; but here is the secret of his success: His inferiority has been transmuted into a burning desire for recognition and fame, the major motive that drives him to work hard, with a spirit of persistence that knows no such word as "impossible."

He is totally without fear! That, too, is the result of a build-up of himself in his own mind, to offset his lack of personality and his recognized inferiority in other ways. He works with a definite goal for every day in the year, and holds himself to a rigid adherence to his self-established sales quota. Of course, he makes the fullest possible use of the Master Mind principle. Otherwise, he has no distinguishing features and no hidden ability. His achievement might be duplicated, with ease, by no fewer than six thousand other life insurance agents who had the same training that this young man received, but neglected or failed to grasp the full meaning and the possibilities of the Master Mind principle.

Reverend Paul Welshimer of Canton, Ohio, made such effective application of the Master Mind principle that he organized the largest Sunday School in America, with a total membership of more than 5,000. His method of applying this principle was both simple and interesting. Briefly described, it consisted of a plan under which he made every member of his church and every member of his Sunday School an active member of his Master Mind. He gave each a part to perform and with it a motive for the faithful performance of the part. He organized both the members of his church and the members of his Sunday School into a series of committees, each of which was given some definite task to perform in connection with the extension of the church influence. The secret of Mr. Welshimer's success might be explained in one brief sentence: "We keep everyone so busy pulling," said he, "that no one has any time or desire to kick."

And the motive which prompted all this harmonious co-operation was nothing more than each member's desire for personal recognition, for work well and faithfully performed. That recognition was given in abundance. The church published its own weekly newspaper, on its own printing press. The paper was devoted entirely to news concerning the members of the church and Sunday School, their work and their social and family activities. That was motive enough to ensure hearty co-operation. Everyone had the thrill of seeing his or her name in the church paper. Those who performed the greatest measure of service had the thrill of seeing their pictures along with their names, occasionally.

"A great preacher!" some will say of Mr. Welshimer. Now, the irony of the whole story is the fact that he can hardly be called a preacher. He is not an able speaker. His sermons usually are dry and uninteresting. He explains his background by saying that prior to his going into the preaching business, he was engaged in the grocery business. But he is a great organiser. There is the real secret of his achievements. He understands the Master Mind principle and works it for all it is worth. His flock does the rest. They do it willingly and have a lot of fun in the bargain. Moreover, they have extended the original, small, one-room church building until it now covers the better portion of a whole city block, including the large public auditorium and the Sunday School rooms it now embraces.

Mr. Welshimer's fame as a churchman has spread far and near, and church and Sunday School leaders have visited his church from nearly every city in America, endeavoring to learn the secret of his success. Well, the "secret" is now the property of any other church leader who wishes to use it. It consists of intelligent application of the Master Mind principle. Nothing else.

Edwin C. Barnes, a business associate of the late Thomas A. Edison, owes much of his success to the unique way in which he applied the Master Mind principle in marketing the Ediphone, the trade name for the Edison dictating machine.

At the time he began the unusual application of this principle, his sales force consisted of about twenty men. He entered into a Master Mind alliance with several firms that were engaged in marketing office furniture and supplies, office labour-saving devices such as adding machines, and typewriters, through which the salesmen representing these firms practically became salesmen of the Ediphone.

The arrangement provided that the salesmen selling the Ediphone and the salesmen representing the office equipment and typewriter firms would exchange favours by supplying one another with the names of prospective purchasers of their respective wares, without expense to anyone.

The plan for carrying out the arrangement was simple, but effective. It consisted of a clearing house carried on by the Barnes organization's telephone switchboard operator, to whom the names of prospective buyers were telephoned daily. In their daily rounds, the salesmen of the office equipment and the typewriter firms kept a close lookout for business firms that might be in need of Ediphones—especially new firms just entering business. These salesmen promptly telephoned the information in to the clearing house.

The salesmen selling Ediphones likewise kept on the lookout for firms that might be in need of any sort of office equipment or typewriters and telephoned the information in. Under this plan, all the firms participating in the Master Mind alliance had the services of a group of sales people who were not on their payrolls, but whose services were nevertheless very profitable.

Ten years of operation under this plan proved to be so successful that Mr. Barnes was able to retire from business, with much more money than he needed and of course the other firms with which he was allied fared equally as well.

Just after the end of World War I, a young woman who had previously been employed as a highly paid private secretary lost her position, because of the failure of the firm for which she worked. She began to look around for another position, but found none that paid the salary she had been accustomed to receiving. While she was searching for a new position, she became a student of the Philosophy of American Achievement.

After hearing but one lecture on the Master Mind principle, she made a discovery that enabled her to create a business of her own from which she earns more than ten times as much as she had previously received as a private secretary.

Her idea was simple enough. Having developed a pleasing "telephone voice" while working as a secretary, she conceived the idea of turning her voice into a profit by supplying certain classes of business firms with duly qualified prospective customers. At first she specialized on supplying prospective buyers of life insurance, automobiles and real estate. Later she added to her list of clients, department stores and other business firms covering a wide range of different classes of business.

Working from the telephone directory, she communicated with every individual listed, procuring from each sufficient information to enable her to determine very accurately those who were prospective customers for her clients. Of course, she had a sales approach for telephone use which enabled her to ascertain precisely for which of her clients an individual might be a prospective customer and her sales talk was designed to qualify every person to whom she talked as being either a likely prospective customer or as not being interested.

One rainy day this clever young woman telephoned me in Washington, D.C., at my home. Speaking in her usual "million-dollar telephone tone of voice," she asked if I would be courteous enough to meet her assistant, Miss Smith, at counter number twelve, in the Men's Department of Woodward and Lothrop's Department Store, where I would be shown something I needed, something she was sure I wanted and something for which I would be sure to thank her. I was agreeable and consented to visit Miss Smith. The young woman's cleverly cultivated voice and expertly prepared sales talk made this visit something for the "must" list. Upon arriving at counter number twelve, I found myself at the end of a lineup of more than a dozen men, all of whom were waiting, along with me, to see what the mysterious Miss Smith had to show them. At the front end of the line Miss Smith was busy enough, fitting rain coats on the men in the waiting line—and selling them too!

The only thing anyone controls completely is his own thoughts. How profoundly significant!

The day's business accounted for the sale of 156 coats, to say nothing of a handsome profit for the clever young woman with the "million dollar voice" who staged it. Every man in the lineup was in an agreeable frame of mind, but one of them bore the brunt of a joke that was unknown to the others. He was the man who trained this young woman in the art of selling by telephone. His name was Napoleon Hill; his coaching of his student on the Master Mind principle had been so complete that she had caught him with his own "bait."

This young woman extended her Master Mind alliance with merchants and business firms by training other young women to qualify by telephone prospective buyers of merchandise until she now has organizations in several of the larger cities. She has no monopoly on the plan. Hence, there is nothing to hinder others from adopting it, as some perhaps have done. I know of a General Agent for a life insurance company who adopted the plan and used it so effectively that he increased the sales of his fifty agents by more than forty percent the first year he put it into operation. He keeps one telephone operator steadily at work, telephoning housewives and arranging with them for his agents to call on their husbands.

To some it may seem quite a jump from the analysis of the business methods of a partner of Thomas A. Edison, to a description of the sales technique of a telephone operator; but the purpose of this chapter is to show how the Master Mind principle may be applied in all occupations from the greatest to the most humble.

I will return, now, to an analysis of the Master Mind as it has been applied by America's most distinguished industrialist, Henry Ford, the man whose astounding achievements were so aptly foretold over thirty years ago by Andrew Carnegie. No attempt will be made to describe all the methods with which Mr. Ford has used the Master Mind, but I will analyse two important applications he made of this principle, both of which are matters of public record.

First I will go back to the year 1914, when Mr. Ford shocked the entire industrial world by announcing that henceforth he would pay all of his day labourers a minimum wage of five dollars per day, regardless of their occupational duties. The prevailing wage, at that time, for similar work performed by a majority of the Ford workers, was about two dollars and a half per day. Other industrial leaders shouted their disapproval of Ford's minimum wage policy and many prophesied that it would drive him into bankruptcy.

Let us take a look at the record and see what effect his policy actually had on his business. Most important of all, perhaps, it cut down his labour cost instead of increasing it, because it had the effect of causing his workers to deliver more service and better service than they had been in the habit of delivering.

It also improved the "mental attitude" in which they worked, thereby raising the morale of the entire works. Out of this new spirit of harmonious cooperation came an understanding between Ford and his men which practically ensured him against labour troubles, since he had already given his men more wages and better working conditions than any labour leader would have had the courage to demand; and be it remembered that more than twenty years later, when labour agitators undertook to break up the spirit of cooperation between Ford and his men, they met with little encouragement.

The Master Mind alliance that Ford established between himself and his men through his minimum wage policy, and in other ways coincidental with that policy, has been one of the strongest factors of his stupendous success, as it was this policy that enabled him to reduce the price of his automobiles down through the years when other manufacturers were increasing the prices of their products.

Long before Ford adopted the Master Mind principle as a means of insuring better cooperation from his workers, he put this principle to use in another direction which had far-reaching repercussions that affected his entire business, and made it possible for him to control his industry without going into the professional money market for operating capital.

The method by which he procured his operating capital was both practical and simple, as have been, in fact, all the Ford methods of doing business. It consisted of a Master Mind alliance between himself and the distributors of his automobiles, through which he arranged for the distributors to obligate themselves each year for a definite number of automobiles which they agreed to buy from him at the wholesale price, and for which they made an advance payment of a certain percentage of the purchase price of each automobile, the remainder payable on delivery of the cars. This advance payment was sufficient to give Ford the necessary working capital with which to produce the automobiles. Therefore, it was unnecessary for him either to borrow money for operating purposes, or to sell stock in his business.

The merchandising value of this method of financing was stupendous, and it consists of a very subtle principle of selling psychology which but few people have ever taken the time to analyze, viz. Ford procured his working capital from the same source that purchased the entire product of his plant. Under this plan his distributors occupied the unique relationship equivalent to a partnership with Ford; a relationship which made his distributors both the purchasers and the salesmen of his entire product, as well as the providers of the necessary working capital with which to manufacture the cars. This strategy in financing relieved Ford of a costly selling job, as well as giving him the operating capital he needed, without subjecting him to the control of professional financiers.

As far as the author knows Ford is the only large-scale industrial operator who has had the vision to correlate the financing of a business with the distribution of its product in such a manner that both these important factors are handled through the same source. This is Master Mind application of great economic importance. The usual orthodox method of financing large industrial and business organizations entirely neglects the famous Ford plan of relating himself to his financiers and the purchasers of his product.

The circumstances of his plan ensure him the fullest cooperation in the management of his business. The usual procedure in the management of industrial operations is to procure working capital from one group of people (generally by the sale of stock), and sell the products of the business to another entirely different group of people.

In this case, the owners of the business have little in common with the people who purchase the product of the business. Under the Ford plan everyone participating in any part of his business has a definite motive for cooperating with him.

It has been said that some of Ford's distributors have complained of his policy of forcing them to purchase a regular quota of automobiles, and pay for a portion of the purchase price in advance. The best reply to this complaint, from the Ford point of view, is the fact that every Ford Distributor's Franchise in the world is an asset that can be turned into money any day; therefore one concludes that the policy under which Ford is related to his distributors must be, on the whole, very profitable to them as well as to himself.

The Ford way of applying the Master Mind principle extends far beyond the alliance he has with his distributors and his immediate workers. It reaches out to nearly all parts of the inhabited portion of the world, and embraces a majority of the millions of men and women who own and drive his automobile.

Through this alliance with the public—and it is a voluntary alliance as far as the public is concerned—Henry Ford probably occupies more friendly space in the minds of the American people than any other living industrialist. This good will asset is a form of riches which cannot be estimated in mere bank balances, automobiles and machinery. It is something which can be converted into cash, at will, and is greater and more enduring than any material thing. If Henry Ford were stripped of every dollar he possesses, and every automobile plant of his were burned to the ground, and if he were left stranded, deprived of every other material thing he possesses, he would still be richer than Croesus, because he could convert his goodwill into all the capital he needed with which to make a comeback, just as quickly as he could send out a call to his millions of friends throughout the world. They would come forth with money, even to their last penny if necessary, and invest it in... in what? Why, they would invest it in their confidence in Henry Ford.

What a lesson this man Ford provides to all who will take the time to find out how and why he has succeeded so abundantly! Most of us look at Ford today, as he stands at the top of the heap of life's fortunes, and see nothing but a man who has been "lucky." If the real truth were known—and it is known to a few—no part of Ford's achievements was due to luck, nor to "favourable breaks," nor to anything else except an intelligent application of the Philosophy of American Achievement.

At Andrew Carnegie's insistent request, the author began, over thirty years ago, to study Henry Ford and his philosophy of life. This personal observation of the automobile king began long before Ford had been recognized as the world's greatest industrial leader. Therefore, I had an opportunity to observe the method, step by step, through which a man starts at scratch, with very little schooling, without any form of public recognition of his outstanding ability, with barely enough money to carry on—and yet lifts himself at long last to the position of number one industrialist in the greatest industrial country in the world.

Because of this extraordinary analysis of Henry Ford, extending as it has, over the major portion of his business life, I have given the students of this philosophy an accurate description of the vital portion of the Ford philosophy which never would have been known without this close scrutiny of the man and his business methods. Nowhere, in any published book concerning Henry Ford, has any writer disclosed what we know to be the real secrets of Henry Ford's astounding success, as they have been described by me.

Henry Ford is not without his deficiencies! Yet it is significant that he has succeeded despite all his mistakes. It is also worthwhile to take note of the fact that his mistakes, as far as the facts are known, seem always to have been on the side of caution and conservatism. It was perhaps a major mistake for him to have delayed changing models of his automobile from time to time, in keeping with the popular trend for streamlined beauty in automobiles, but his ability to recover from the results of his mistakes was so great that he absorbed the losses due to his mistakes, without seriously impairing his fortune or disturbing his harmonious relationship with the public and its confidence in him.

I turn, now, from the description of the Master Mind principle, as it has been and may be applied in sundry occupations, and introduce Dr. Elmer R. Gates and Dr. Alexander Graham Bell, the great American scientists to whom Andrew Carnegie sent me for collaborative aid in the organization of the Philosophy of American Achievement. The achievements of these two men are too well-known to most of the people of America to make necessary a detailed description of their work. Dr. Bell was the inventor of the long distance telephone, and had to his credit other accomplishments of great value to mankind. Dr. Gates had to his credit patents on more inventions than any other American inventor, not excepting Thomas A. Edison and Dr. Bell. He specialized in the study of mental phenomena, and made valuable contributions to the altogether too meager stock of knowledge the world has acquired on this subject.

Over a period of more than three years these distinguished men collaborated with me in the organization of this philosophy, providing me with all they had learned of the mysteries of the human mind. Except for Andrew Carnegie's foresight in having sent me to study under these two men, the major portion of their priceless discoveries in connection with the operation of the mind would have been lost to the world, for neither of them left more than mere fragmentary portions of their discoveries in condition for use by others. Even these were in terms that made the information understandable only to men of science.

I now introduce Dr. Elmer R. Gates, who speaks for both himself and Dr. Bell, and give you his analysis of the Master Mind and other principles of mind operation, as nearly as possible in his own terminology, just as he described them to me.

Hill: Mr. Carnegie sent me to you, Dr. Gates, to request your cooperation in providing the people of America with a practical, workable philosophy of individual achievement based on the experiences of business and industrial leaders, and the discoveries of men of science, such as yourself. Will you, therefore, go ahead and give me the story of the highlights of your research in the field of mental phenomena, bearing in mind that you are speaking for the benefit of men and women many of whom have not had an opportunity to acquire scientific knowledge of psychology; and some whose schooling, for the most part, has not extended beyond the high school?

Dr. Gates: You have given me a sizable order, but I will fill it to the best of my ability. Where shall we begin?

Hill: First of all, I would like to compare notes with you on the subject of the Master Mind principle which Mr. Carnegie described as the major source of all his achievements. He defined this principle as "Coordination of two or more minds, working in perfect harmony for the attainment of a definite purpose." As Mr. Carnegie explained this principle, it appears to be the only known medium of contact through which one may use the great reservoir of spiritual power available to mankind, as well as the principle through which one individual may appropriate and use the knowledge, experience, education, and strategic, imaginative capacity of others.

Dr. Gates: Yes, I know exactly what you want. Dr. Bell and I have spent many years experimenting with this principle. Of course, I will be happy to give you the full benefit of all we have learned about it; but I must caution you, at the outset, not to jump at any conclusions in connection with your study of this subject until you have acquired a complete picture of all that has been learned about it. Neither Dr. Bell nor I can claim to have acquired more than surface knowledge of this subject, but we have gone far enough to convince ourselves that it opens the way of approach to a source of knowledge that cannot be drawn upon or used except through its application. Also, we have come to the conclusion that civilization will never reach its highest goal until knowledge of the Master Mind principle is the common property of all the people of the world.

Do not become alarmed at this warning, for I hope to give you what information I have acquired on the subject of the Master Mind, in terms that anyone may understand.

First, perhaps I should explain what I believe to be the two features of major interest in connection with the Master Mind principle, viz.:

(a) When two or more minds are brought together and their forces are combined, for the attainment of a definite objective, the combination has the effect of stimulating each individual mind so it becomes more alert, more imaginative and more active in the use of faith, than an individual experiences when his mind functions independently. This fact (and we know, beyond room for the slightest doubt, that it is a fact) is of the utmost importance, because it suggests a practical approach by which an individual may supplement the powers of his own mind with a form of intelligence that recognizes no limitations. The extra stimulation of the mind which each individual experiences, through this sort of harmonious alliance with other minds, may be greatly increased by the simple procedure of discussion of the object of the alliance, and any form of action leading to the attainment of the purpose of the alliance. It appears that a meeting of the minds of individuals, accompanied by definite action for the purpose of achieving some definite objective, has the effect of developing in each individual the necessary faith to lead to success.

It was this sort of an alliance of minds which gave birth to the determined spirit that drove George Washington's armies to win against overwhelming odds. And it is this sort of alliance of minds that gives our American form of government its stupendous power to maintain and defend itself against all foes. It is also the same sort of alliance that has established the great industrial system of America, our banking system, and the other institutions that distinguish ours from all other countries.

(b) The other feature of the Master Mind extends far beyond one's relationship with the material circumstances and things of life, and brings the individual within easy reach of the forces of Infinite Intelligence, from which and through which one may tap a source of knowledge which appears to embrace all of Nature's laws! It seems that this source of super knowledge becomes available only to those individuals who are inspired and motivated by a desire to help mankind, raise himself to a higher standard of intelligence, and it is never reached by those motivated only by the desire for personal aggrandizement in connection with material things. For evidence of the soundness of this theory (and mind you, I claim for it nothing more than a theory) take notice of the regularity with which the scientist, who deals entirely with laws governing material things, comes to the end of the trail, where he is stopped by a stone wall beyond which physical laws cannot carry him. Only the philosopher, the metaphysician, and the individual who discards his physical laws for the higher law of faith seems to be able to scale that wall. At times I have assumed the role of both the scientist who follows the lead of physical laws, and the philosopher who goes beyond the dead end wall, with faith as his guide; therefore I have the right to speak from personal observation when I say that there is a source of knowledge that is available to mankind through no approach other than faith.

And it may be well if we here define faith as a, "state of mind in which an individual discards all limitations of his own reason, or will power, and opens wide his mind for divine guidance of his efforts toward the achievement of a definite objective."

My experiments with the Master Mind principle have convinced me that an individual working through harmony with other minds, can more quickly reach that state of mind wherein he projects his mind power beyond the bounds of his reason and will, than he can when he moves independently. Even the animals of a lower order of intelligence, such as a dog, gain courage and initiative when driven by the spirit of the pack. A dog, for example, may never think of killing a sheep on its own initiative; but let that same dog join in a pack of dogs whose leader is bent on sheep killing and it will engage in the activity viciously and without hesitation. This same tendency may be found among boys, and of course it obtains as well among men. Mass effort, team work, collaboration between men who move together in a spirit of harmony, give an individual an incentive to action which comes from no other source.

There is still another feature of the Master Mind principle worthy of analysis. It is the fact that an individual whose mind has been "stepped up" through contact with other minds in a Master Mind meeting becomes conscious of a form of mind stimulation which amounts to intoxication, and this condition lasts often for many hours after the meeting ends. The mind, when acting under this form of intoxication, falls easily and naturally into that state of openness wherein the state of mind known as faith begins to manifest itself. For evidence of this, observe the state of mind of salesmen who have attended a sales "pep" meeting, where some dynamic leader worked the group up to a high pitch of enthusiasm, and you will notice that every salesman carries away with him a definite amount of courage far above that which he had when he entered the meeting. Here you have the cue by which successful sales managers get results. The man who knows best how to establish a spirit of rapport between the minds of his salesmen is always the ablest manager of salesmen, although he, himself, may be a very poor salesman. Here, too, is the cue to all men in all walks of life who wish to project their own influence in any calling, through alliance with other minds. Not always is the clergyman who can preach the most interesting sermon the best church leader. The real leader is the man who can best bring his followers together in a spirit of harmonious cooperation through which he induces them to think and act as one mind.

Take Andrew Carnegie, for example. Analyze his personality, study his educational background, and weigh him as you will. In the end, you will be forced to the conclusion that in most respects he is only an average man. Observe his method of relating himself to the members of his Master Mind group and here you will find the secret of his power. He knows how to get men to form a composite mind and work together as one, subordinating entirely their own personal interests and ideas for the benefit of the group. Here is the entire secret of Carnegie's astounding success as a leader of industry. He would be just as effective a leader in any other field of endeavour as he is in the steel business, for he has discovered that the secret of all great personal power lies in the harmonious alliance of minds.

Hill: You say, Dr. Gates, that an individual who becomes mentally stimulated through association with other minds, in a Master Mind meeting, carries the effects of the stimulation with him for some time after the meeting. Do you mean that an individual's mind becomes and remains more alert for a time, so he may use his mind more effectively after subjecting it to the Master Mind influence, even though he acts independently?

Dr. Gates: Yes, I mean just that. In some instances this stimulation lasts only a few hours. In other instances, it may last several days, and in rare cases, several weeks.

Hill: Then it is necessary for the leader of a Master Mind group to keep in close contact with the members of his alliance, if he is to get the desired benefits from the alliance?

Dr. Gates: Oh yes! by all means. Observe with what regularity Mr. Carnegie and other business leaders of his calibve meet with their staff members. Neglect in this respect will render the Master Mind alliance impotent. It must not be assumed that because a man is associated with others he will get the full benefit of their minds unless he keeps in almost continuous contact with those minds and keeps his alliance active through discussion, planning, and action! Here, as everywhere else throughout Nature's world, the law of life is development and growth through use! Nature discourages vacuums and inaction. The best minds are those that are used the most.

Hill: Is it true, or not, Dr. Gates, that Andrew Carnegie, Thomas A. Edison, and others of their recognized standing in their respective fields of endeavour, were born with brain capacity superior to that of the average person? Is this not the reason why they have surpassed the majority of men?

The whole world willingly follows the man who shows by his actions that he knows precisely where he is going.

Dr. Gates: Your question cannot be answered intelligently without safeguarding the answer with many modifications, ifs, buts and maybes! Let me answer it the only way it can be truthfully answered, first categorically, by saying that the complex and mysterious machinery of the human brain is such that no one has ever yet been smart enough to analyze any brain by any set standard of measurement of its capabilities. We know that a man like Thomas A. Edison came into this world with a brain that was seemingly so subnormal that his school teachers sent him home, after three months of apparently futile effort to teach him the simple fundamentals of a common school education, with the dictum that he "hadn't enough sense to take an education." In the light of this true story, we are forced, by the demonstrations of power he gave the world through that same brain later on, to admit that about all we really know of the brain is that we know nothing at all! By this I do not mean either to be facetious or to evade your question. I intend only to be honest. However, I would not be quite fair if I did not call attention to the equally significant fact that nature sometimes brings into the world individuals whose capacity to absorb knowledge (from the very tender years of childhood) forces the world to recognize them as prodigies. I would say that every brain in this class has possibilities of development and use far surpassing anything the average brain ever attains. Take the individuals under this classification who rise to unusual heights of achievement, analyze them carefully, and you will be impressed by the fact that they owe their achievements to the stimulus of some motive which caused them to take charge of their minds and use them intensely.

Hill: You are now coming pretty close to answering the question that interests me very keenly. This question doubtlessly will interest many others who are trying to make better use of their native abilities in the solution of life's far-flung and complex problems. That question is: Where and what is the starting point from which one may begin to take charge of his own mind so he can make better use of it in the business of earning a living?

Dr. Gates: The beginning of all achievement is Definiteness of Purpose based on the right motive or incentive to influence one to put forth extraordinary effort!

Hill: That is a mighty brief answer for such an important question, Dr. Gates. Can you expand it so your answer will become a more definite guide for the man who is trying to find a place at which he can take a hold on his own mind?

Dr. Gates: I could extend the answer into voluminous words and illustrations, but I doubt that I could improve it. The truth is this: A man can accomplish about whatever he makes up his mind to do.

The extent to which he makes up his mind is entirely a matter of motive. It is far more important for a man to become deeply inspired with a definite motive than it is for him to be brilliant, or that he be highly educated. Motive gives men vision, imagination, and initiative, self-reliance, and Definiteness of Purpose. With these qualities of mind—plus the use of the Master Mind principle through which an individual may borrow the education, experience and ability of others—a man may lift himself above all limitations and attain just about any objective he sets out to attain.

One thing is certain. There is nothing to indicate that the majority of men of great financial and business achievement are anything but average men as far as their brain capacities and intelligence are concerned. Study these men, wherever you find them, and be convinced of this truth. The thing called genius usually is a myth. Upon close observation, so-called genius often turns out to be nothing but Definiteness of Purpose backed by strong motive.

Hill: Your statements are rather astounding, Dr. Gates. They are also quite reassuring to us who recognize that we are only average people, especially those of us who have acquired but little schooling. May I quote you on all you have said?

Dr. Gates: By all means quote me! It might help if all men got over this false belief that success is for the few; that those few are blessed with some mysterious form of superior ability. I am no authorized agent to speak for the Creator, but I cannot help thinking that if He had not intended for the blessings of the world to be appropriated and used by the "average man" he would not have made so many average men!

And I am, by experience, impressed with the inescapable fact that the greatest achievements known to civilization have been the handiwork of average men! As paradoxical as it may seem, I must call attention to the fact that a truly great man is only an average man who has discovered his own mind and has taken charge of it.

I hope that my frankness will not disillusion you. If you came to me with the expectation of hearing me say that genius is born and not made through discovery and use of one's mind, that is the very thought I wish to discourage.

Every adversity is a blessing in disguise, provided it teaches some lesson we would not have learned without it.

Hill: You have agreeably surprised me, Dr. Gates; but you have not disillusioned me, for I came to you with the hope that I might learn, from your experiments in connection with the operation of the mind, exactly what you have told me. I shall be happy to give reassurance, to every person who becomes a student of the philosophy of achievement, that you are right when you say Definiteness of Purpose, backed by an intense motive, is more important than brilliancy of mind. Coming, as it has, from a man of your wide range of experiments in connection with the power of the mind, this statement may give hope and purpose to many who otherwise might despair of the hope of personal achievement.

This concluded my interview with Dr. Gates, and his observations are a fitting testimonial to the power of the Master Mind Principle, and a fitting conclusion to this chapter.

Nothing brings enduring happiness except that which helps others to find it.

□

Chapter Three

Going the Extra Mile

It is a well-established fact that men who make themselves indispensable in any job, business or profession generally write their own price tag and the world willingly pays it.

This chapter covers a subject which, more than all others, describes the method by which one may make himself indispensable. Therefore, the chapter may be of priceless value to all readers who earn their living by rendering service to others.

Reduced to its simplest terms, Going the extra mile means the rendering of more service and better service than one is paid to render. When adopted and followed as a habit, this principle gives one the benefit of the law of increasing returns. Stated conversely, failure to apply this principle as a habit, handicaps one through the operation of the law of diminishing returns.

A man who has been prominently engaged in the business of helping men and women to market their personal services to best advantages once said that a strict observance of the habit of doing more than one is paid to do is one unbeatable method by which an individual may promote himself to whatever position he is capable of filling.

Inasmuch as Andrew Carnegie founded the largest industrial organization in the United States, the great United States Steel Corporation, and during his business career became one of the largest employers of men, his views on the subject of this chapter should be of great help to the reader.

Not only was Mr. Carnegie one of the largest employers of men, but it is a well-known fact that he was one of America's keenest judges of men. It is believed that he helped his men, relate themselves to one another and to the business so efficiently that he made more millionaires than any other American industrialist, therefore he became an authority on the ways and means by which men market their service to best advantage.

It is worthy of note, also, that all the more than 500 distinguished leaders in industry and business who collaborated in the organization of the Philosophy of American Achievement emphasized the value of rendering more service and better service than one is paid to render by scrupulously following this habit themselves.

I call attention to these facts at the beginning of this chapter because of the wide spread and growing tendency of people in America to reverse this principle by rendering as little service and as poor service as they can get away with.

Economic law makes it impossible for any man over a long period of time to take out of a job or commercial enterprise more than he puts into it. This law is not a man-made law entirely. It has its roots in the laws of nature, as there is evidence everywhere in the realm of nature that nature frowns upon the attempt to get something for nothing, or anything for less than its value.

Those who respond to this admonition are sure to discover that sooner or later they will be rewarded adequately for their wisdom, and the reward will consist of their receiving compensation far greater than the actual value of the services they render. The compensation will consist, not only of material gain, but it will be evidenced by greater strength of character, improved mental attitude and the development of self-reliance, initiative, enthusiasm and a reputation that will create an enduring market for their service.

There is a growing tendency on the part of a large number of people in America toward the habit of trying to get something for nothing. This dangerous trend began at the end of the First World War. It has been so definitely intensified during recent years that it now threatens to undermine the entire American way of life.

This trend has already begun to whittle away at the foundation of American industry, which is the main source of employment.

No industry can operate successfully where men group themselves together in blocs and, by sheer strength of their numbers, or coercion, force the wage scales upward, and the quality and the quantity of service they perform, downward. There is a point beyond which this practice cannot be carried without bankrupting industry, and that point has just about been reached.

As this chapter is being written America faces the greatest crisis since that which gave this nation birth, 165 years ago. We are in the beginning of a great National Defense Program which is dependent, entirely, upon American industry. The program cannot be success carried out by men who selfishly demand a full day's pay for a poor day's labour.

If there has ever been a time when every loyal American should do more than he is paid for, that time is now. The present emergency demands that the people of America forget their selfish interests and throw themselves wholeheartedly into the job of saving their right to liberty and freedom.

The time is at hand when every citizen is called upon to do more than he is paid for, not merely to promote his own private interests, but to contribute his part toward saving the American form of democracy which provides us all with our privilege of individual liberty and freedom.

The habit of Going the Extra Mile is, and always has been, the very hub of all personal promotion. No noteworthy success has ever been attained without following this habit. But the time has come, now, when we must go the extra mile to save the institution of Americanism.

If we wish to continue our enjoyment of a system of government that has given us the highest standard of living known to civilization, we must protect the foundation stones of that government and make them secure. This is a task which makes it not only desirable for us to Go the Extra Mile, but an absolute necessity.

Those of us who lack the ambition to do more than we are paid for as a means of self-promotion must adopt this habit as a means of self-protection. We may not wish personal luxury, but we surely have not sunk so low that we do not want personal liberty.

Liberty, like everything else that is worth having, has a price. We cannot buy liberty by doing as little as possible and demanding in return for this the fruits of liberty. No, the time is at hand when the American people will either take up and apply the spirit of the pioneers who risked their lives and their fortunes to give us liberty, or find themselves once more under the bondage of a foreign dictatorship which knows nothing of justice and liberty.

On this there can be no half way point, no appeasement, no compromise. We have our backs to the wall and there is only one way in which we can move, and that calls for our Going the Extra Mile, in a spirit of determination which knows no such reality as failure.

We cannot remain "the richest and freest country in the world" without paying for the privilege. There is no such thing as something for nothing. We either pay for what we want or take what is forced upon us!

Therefore, as you read this chapter, take it to heart and make up your mind to go the extra mile in support of something far more profound than the promotion of your own private interests.

Meanwhile, in so doing you will have learned a great lesson in self-promotion which will serve you the remainder of your life, just as it has served Andrew Carnegie and all others who have converted American opportunity into personal riches.

> Render more service and better service than you agree to render and very soon you will be willingly paid for more than you actually do.

Hidden behind the lines of this lesson is a secret of achievement which was uncovered by Andrew Carnegie and revealed to the man through whom he asked that the secret be given only to those who are known to have other qualities essential for success without which it might be dangerous.

This same secret was known to successful men who contributed to the organization of this philosophy. It is not likely that any reader will uncover the secret except by the habit of Going the Extra Mile, in which event it will reveal itself somewhere along the way, perhaps at some unexpected time and place.

Early one frosty morning, some twenty-odd years ago, the private railroad car of Charles M. Schwab was shifted to the side track at his steel plant, in Pennsylvania.

As he left the car he was met by a young man who explained that he was a stenographer in the office of the steel company and he had met the car with the hope that he might be of some service to Mr. Schwab.

"Who requested you to meet me here?" Schwab asked.

"It was my own idea, Sir," the young man replied, "and I knew you were coming on the early morning train because I handled a telegram that stated you were coming. I brought my notebook with me, Sir; and I'll be glad to take any letters or telegrams you may wish to send."

Mr. Schwab thanked the young man for his thoughtfulness, but said he needed no service at the moment, although he might send for the lad later in the day. And he did! When the private car returned to New York that night it carried that young man to the city, where he had been assigned, at Mr. Schwab's request, for duty in the steel magnate's private office.

The young man's name is Williams. Mr. Williams promoted himself from one job to another in the steel organization until he earned and saved enough money to enable him to go into business for himself, and he later founded a drug company of which he is the president and majority shareholder.

Nothing very dramatic or interesting about this brief story is there?

Well, the answer depends altogether upon what one calls drama. To every man who is trying to find his place in the world, this story, if analyzed carefully, carries the deepest sort of drama, for it describes the practical application of one of the more important of the principles of individual achievement: the habit of Going the Extra Mile!

I said that this young man promoted himself from one job to another in the steel company. Let us find out how he managed this self-promotion in order that we may learn how others can profit by his technique. Let us learn, if we can, what young Williams had in the way of ability which other stenographers in the general plant operation office of the steel company did not have, that caused him to be singled out by Mr. Schwab and assigned to his personal service.

We have Mr. Schwab's own word that young Williams did not possess a single quality that entitled him to rate above the average as a stenographer, but he did have one quality; a quality that he developed on his own initiative and practiced as an inviolable habit, which but few people possess, and that was the habit of rendering more service and better service than he was paid for.

It was this habit that enabled him to promote himself! It was this habit that attracted the attention of Mr. Schwab. It was this habit that helped him to become the head of a corporation where he became his own Boss.

And it was this habit which, many years previous to the incident here related, brought Mr. Schwab, himself, to the attention of Mr. Carnegie and gained for him his opportunity to promote himself into a position in which he became his own Boss.

It was also this same habit that enabled the irrepressible Carnegie to rise from the position of day labourer to that of the owner of America's largest industry, where he accumulated a vast fortune in money and a still greater fortune in useful knowledge.

Mr. Carnegie's views on the subject of Going the Extra Mile provide the reader with a practical working technique with which he may use this principle effectively for his own self-promotion. His analysis of the subject is here presented in his own words, just as he explained it to the author at the beginning of the organization of the philosophy of individual achievement, viz.:

Hill: Mr. Carnegie, I have heard some men express the belief that success often is the result of luck. Many people seem to believe that successful men achieve their success because they get the favourable "breaks" of life, and that others fail because they get the unfavourable "breaks."

Croesus, the wealthy Persian philosopher, made some such reference to chance when he said:

"There is a Wheel on which the affairs of men revolve, and its mechanism is such that it prevents any man from being always fortunate."

Have you, in the richness of your business experience, seen any evidence of such a wheel? Do you attribute any portion of your success to luck, or favourable "breaks?"

Carnegie: Your questions give me a suitable starting point for an appropriate description of the habit of Going the Extra Mile, by which I mean the habit of rendering more service and better service than one is paid for.

First, I will answer your question by saying yes, indeed, there is a wheel of life that controls human destinies, and I am happy to be able to tell you that this wheel can be definitely influenced to operate in one's favour. If this were not true there would be no object in organizing the rules of personal achievement.

Hill: Will you tell me, in the simplest words possible, just how one may control this wheel of fortune? I would like a description of this important success factor which the young man or young woman just beginning a business career may understand.

Carnegie: I will describe the particular rule of success which will, if properly applied, enable a person literally to write his own price tag, with more than an average chance of getting that which he desires. Moreover, this rule is so potent that it practically ensures one against serious opposition from those who purchase his services. As I have already stated, this rule is known as the habit of Going the Extra Mile, which means the habit of doing more than one is paid to do. You will observe that I have injected an important word into the description of this rule: the word habit!

Before the application of the rule begins to bring back appreciable results it must become a habit, and it must be applied at all times, in all possible ways. It means that one must render the greatest amount of service of which he is capable, and he must render it in a friendly, harmonious manner. Moreover, he must do this regardless of the amount of the immediate compensation he receives and even if he receives no immediate compensation whatsoever.

Hill: But, Mr. Carnegie, most of the people I know, those who work for wages or a salary, claim that they are already doing more work than that for which they are paid. If this is true why aren't they doing a better job of influencing the wheel of fortune on their behalf than they appear to be doing? Why aren't they rich, as you are?

Carnegie: The answer to your question is simple enough, but it has many angles I shall have to explain before you'll understand it. In the first place, if you will accurately analyze those who work for wages you will learn that 98 out of every hundred have no Definite Major Purpose greater than that of working for a daily wage. Therefore, no matter how much work they do, or how well they do it, the wheel of fortune will turn on past them without providing more than a bare living, because they neither expect nor demand more. Ponder over this truth for a moment and you will be better prepared to follow the logic I will present in the remainder of this discussion.

The major difference between those who accept a limitation of daily wages sufficient only for a bare living, and myself, is this: I demand riches in definite terms; I have a definite plan for acquiring riches; I am engaged in carrying out my plan, and I am giving an equivalent, in useful service, of the value of those riches I demand, while the others have no such plan or purpose.

Life is paying me off on my own terms. It is doing precisely the same thing for the man who asks no more than daily wages. You see, the wheel of fortune follows the mental blueprint that a man sets up in his own mind, and it brings back to him, in physical or financial measure, an exact equivalent of that blueprint.

Unless you grasp the full meaning of this statement of truth you will miss the important portion of this discussion. There is a law of compensation through the operation of which a man may establish his own relationship with life, including the material possessions he accumulates. There is no escape from the acceptance of the reality of this law, for it is not a man-made law.

Hill: I can understand your viewpoint, Mr. Carnegie. Stating the matter in another way, may we not say that every man is where he is and what he is because of the use he makes of his own mind?

Carnegie: You have stated the idea correctly. The major difficulty of most men who go through life poverty-stricken is that they neither recognize the power of their own minds nor make any attempt to take possession of their minds. That which a man can accomplish with his hands seldom brings more than a mere living. That which a man can accomplish through the use of his mind may give him whatever he asks of life.

Now let us get on with our analysis of the principle of Going the Extra Mile. I am going to explain some of the more practical advantages of this principle. I call them practical because they are benefits of which anyone may avail himself, without the consent of others.

Let us consider, first, the fact that the habit of doing more than one is paid for brings one to the favourable attention of those who have opportunities to offer. I have never yet known of any man promoting himself to a higher and more profitable position without adopting and following this habit.

The habit aids one in developing and maintaining the right "mental attitude" toward others, thereby serving as an effective means of gaining friendly cooperation.

It helps one to profit by the law of contrast, since obviously a majority of the people follow the exact opposite of this principle, by doing just as little work as they can get by with; and that is about all they are getting; just getting by!

It creates a continuous market for one's services. Moreover, it ensures one a choice of jobs and working conditions, at the top of the scale of wages or other forms of compensation.

It attracts opportunities which are not available to those who render as little service as possible, and thereby serves as an effective medium for self-promotion from wage earning to business ownership.

Under some circumstances it enables one to become indispensable in his job, thereby paving the way for his naming his own compensation.

It aids one in the development of self-reliance.

Most important of all its benefits, it gives one the advantage of the law of increasing returns through which he will eventually receive compensation far beyond the actual market value of the service he renders. Therefore, the habit of doing more than one is paid for is a sound business principle, even if it is used purely as a measure of expediency, to promote one's personal interests advantageously.

The habit of doing more than one is paid for is one that an individual may practice without asking the permission of others; therefore it is under one's own control. Many other beneficial habits can be practiced only through the consent and the cooperation of other people.

Hill: Mr. Carnegie, do all the men who work for you have your permission to render more service and better service than that for which they are paid, and if so, how many are taking advantage of this privilege in a manner that is beneficial to themselves?

Carnegie: I'm glad you asked that question, because it gives me an opportunity to drive home an important viewpoint on this subject. First, let me say that every person working for me (and this applies with equal truth to all who have worked for me in the past) not only has the privilege of doing more than he is being paid for, but I encourage all who work for me to do this very thing, for their benefit as well as my own.

It may surprise you to hear that of the many thousands of men who work for me, but a very small number have taken the trouble to place me under obligations to them by rendering more service and better service than that for which they are paid. Among the few exceptions are members of our supervisory and managerial groups, and every one of them is receiving compensation far greater than that received by the majority of our workers, although every man in my employ has the privilege of rendering this sort of service without asking the consent of anyone.

Some of the members of my Master Mind group, such men as Charles Schwab, have made themselves so definitely indispensable to our business that they have earned as much as a million dollars in one year, over and above their fixed salaries. Not a few of the men who have thus promoted themselves into the higher brackets of income in our organization have attracted opportunities to go into business for themselves.

Hill: Couldn't you have driven a better bargain with those to whom you paid as much as a million dollars a year in extra compensation?

Carnegie: Oh, to be sure I could have had their services for much less money, but you must remember that this principle of doing more than one is paid for operates in favour of an employer just the same as it operates for the benefit of the employee. Therefore, it is just as much an act of wisdom for an employer to pay a man all he earns as it is for an employee to endeavour to earn more than he receives. By paying Charlie Schwab all he earned I thereby ensured myself against the loss of his services.

Hill: You speak of paying your men who render more service than they are paid for, all they earn. If you do that, how can they render more service then they are paid for? It seems that there is an inconsistency in your statement.

Carnegie: That which you mistake for inconsistency is the only mistake of many others on this subject, and is due to a lack of understanding of the habit of Going the Extra Mile. The apparent inconsistency is, therefore, an illusion, but I am glad you asked the question because I will set you right on this subject. It is a fact that I pay my men all they earn, even though I sometimes have to pay them huge sums, but there is one important point that you have overlooked. It is the fact that before I begin paying them all they earn they must establish their indispensability by doing more than they are paid for.

Now, here is the fine point that most people overlook. Until a man begins to render more service than that for which he is paid he is not entitled to more pay than he receives for that service, since obviously he is already receiving full pay for what he does.

I think I can make the point clear by calling attention to the simple illustration of the farmer. Before he collects pay for his services he carefully and intelligently prepares the soil, plows and harrows it, fertilizes it if need be, then plants it with seed.

Up to this point he has gained nothing whatsoever for his labour, but, understanding the law of growth, as he does, he rests after his labour while nature germinates the seed and yields him a crop.

Here the element of time enters into the farmer's labour. In due time, nature gives him back the seed he planted in the ground, together with an abundant overplus to compensate him for his labour and his knowledge. If he sows a bushel of wheat in properly prepared soil he gets back the bushel of seed, together with perhaps as many as ten additional bushels as his compensation.

Here the law of increasing returns has stepped in and compensated the farmer for his labour and his intelligence. If there were no such law man could not exist on this earth, since obviously there would be no object in planting a bushel of wheat in the ground if nature yielded back only a bushel of grain. It is this overplus which nature yields, through the law of increasing returns, that makes it possible for man to produce from the ground the food needed for both man and beast.

But little imagination is needed to see that the man who renders more service and better service than that for which he is paid thereby places himself in a position to benefit by this same law.

If a man rendered only as much service as he is paid to render, then he would have no logical reason to expect or demand more than the fair value of that service.

One of the evils of today is the attempt, on the part of someone, to reverse this rule and collect more pay than the value of the service they render. Some men endeavour to force down the hours of labour and boost up the rate of pay. This practice cannot be pursued indefinitely. When men continue to collect more for their labour than the value of their services, they ultimately exhaust the source of their own wages, and the sheriff makes the next move.

I want you to understand this point clearly, because lack of knowledge on this subject is destined to bring ruin to the American system of industry if the practice of endeavouring to receive more for labour than one puts into it is not corrected. The man to do the correcting is the man who depends upon his labour for a living, for he is the only man who has the privilege of initiative in the correction of this unsound practice.

Please do not misunderstand me to be speaking disparagingly of the man who earns his living from daily labour, for the truth is that I am endeavouring to aid the labouring man by giving him a sounder philosophy of relationship in connection with the marketing of his services.

Hill: If I understand you correctly, Mr. Carnegie, you believe it would be just as unwise for an employer to withhold from an employee any portion of the wages he had justly earned, as it would be for an employee to set up a handicap for himself by doing less than he is paid to do. And I reach the conclusion, from what you have said, that your reasoning on this entire subject is based on your understanding of sound economics and the principle of increasing returns.

Carnegie: You have grasped the idea perfectly, and allow me to congratulate you, because most people never seem to understand the great potential benefits available to those who follow the habit of rendering more service than that for which they are paid.

Often I have heard working men say, "I'm not paid to do that;" or, "This is not my responsibility;" and "I'll be blankety-blank if I'll do anything I'm not paid for." You've heard statements like that. Everyone has.

Well, when you hear a man talking like this you may mark him down as one who never will get more than a bare living from his work. Moreover, that sort of "mental attitude" makes one disliked by his associates, and it therefore discourages favourable opportunities for self-promotion.

When I go in search of a man to fill a responsible position, the very first quality I look for is that of a positive, agreeable mental attitude. You may wonder why I do not look first for ability to do the work I want done. I'll tell you why! The man with a negative mental attitude will disturb the harmony of relationship of all with whom he works; therefore, he is a disintegrating influence which no efficient manager wants to deal with. I look first for the right mental attitude also because where this is found one generally finds along with it a willingness to learn. Then the ability necessary to do a certain job can be developed.

When Charlie Schwab first went to work for me he had no ability as far as surface appearances went, other than that possessed by any other day labourer. But Charlie had an unbeatable mental attitude and a disarming personality that enabled him to win friends among all classes of men.

He also had a natural willingness to do more than he was paid for. This quality was so pronounced in him that he actually went out of his way to get into the way of work. He not only went the extra mile, but he added two or three extra miles, and went with a smile upon his face and the right attitude in his heart.

He also went in a hurry and came back for more when he had finished any task assigned to him. He took hold on a hard job as eagerly as a hungry man takes on food when it is set before him.

Now, what can one do with a man like that, except to give him plenty of rein and let him go as fast as he pleases? That sort of mental attitude inspires confidence. It also attracts opportunities that would run away from the man who carries a frown on his face and a grouch in his heart.

I tell you frankly that there is no way to hold back a man with that sort of mental attitude. He writes his own price tag and gets it willingly. If one employer is short-sighted enough to withhold recognition of such a man, through adequate compensation, some wiser employer will soon discover him and give him a better job. The law of supply and demand, therefore, steps in and forces the proper reward for such a man. The employer has very little to do about such circumstances. The initiative is entirely in the hands of the employee.

Nor is this example of the wisdom of rendering more service than one is paid for applicable only to the relationship of employer and employee. The same rules apply with equal definiteness to professional men; in fact to all who make their living by serving others. The grocer who tilts the scales in favour of the customer when he is weighing a pound of sugar is wiser, by far, than the grocer who waters his sugar to make it weigh more.

The merchant who "rounds down" and gives the customer the odd half cent, in making change, instead of taking it himself, is wiser by far than the merchant who refuses to do this. I have known merchants to lose the business of customers worth hundreds of dollars a year by this pinch-penny habit that some merchants have, of taking the odd half cent in making change.

I once knew a little merchant who went up and down the Monongahela Valley, near Pittsburgh, peddling his merchandise from a pack that he carried on his back. I have heard it said that the pack weighed more than the man who carried it.

When the merchant made a sale he usually threw in some extra article that had not been paid for, as an expression of his gratitude for the patronage given him. Oh, the gift did not amount to much as far as its monetary value was concerned, but he made it with such a pleasant mental attitude that the customer always spoke of the courtesy to all the neighbours, thereby giving the merchant free publicity he could not have purchased with money alone.

In a little while this merchant disappeared from his established route. His customers began to make enquiries as to what had happened to him. The enquiries were prompted by a genuine affection for "the little man with the big pack," as they called him.

Within a few months the little man showed up again. This time he came without his big pack. He came to tell all his customers that he had opened a store of his own in Pittsburgh.

> If you do not render more services than that for which you are paid, you are already getting all you're worth, and you've no right to ask for more.

That store is now one of the largest and most prosperous in the city. It is known as the Horn Department Store, founded and owned by "the little man with the big pack" and, one might add, "the little man with the big heart and the wise brain."

We look at men who have "arrived" and say "how fortunate" or "how lucky." All too often we fail to enquire into the source of their "luck," for if we did we might learn that their luck consisted of their habit of rendering more service and better service than they were paid for, as in the case of "the little man with the big pack."

Word has reached my ears, many times, that Charlie Schwab got a favourable "break" because old man Carnegie took a fancy to him and pushed him up front, ahead of all the others. The truth is that Charlie pushed himself up front. All I had to do in the matter was to keep out of his way and let him go. Any favourable "break" that he received he created for himself, through his own initiative.

When you describe this principle in the philosophy of individual achievement be sure to emphasize what I have told you about it, because it is the one safe and sure rule through which anyone may influence the wheel of life so it will yield benefits that will more than offset any misfortunes it may bring.

When you take the philosophy to the world be sure to tell the people how to use this principle of doing more than they are paid for, as a definite means of making themselves indispensable to those whom they serve. Be sure, also, to explain that this is the success rule through which the Law of Compensation can be deliberately put into operation in one's behalf.

I have always thought it was a great tragedy that Emerson did not explain more clearly, in his essay on Compensation, that the habit of rendering more service and better service than one is paid for has the effect of placing the Law of Compensation back of one's efforts.

Hill: Do you know of successful men who do not follow the habit of doing more than they are paid for?

Carnegie: I know of no successful man, in any calling or business, who does not follow this habit either consciously or unconsciously. Study any successful man, regardless of his vocation, and you will learn quickly enough that he does not work by the clock.

If you study carefully those who let their picks hang in the air the moment the whistle blows for quitting time, you will learn that they are making nothing but a bare living.

Find me one person who is an exception to this rule and I'll give you a check for a thousand dollars, on the spot, provided that this man will permit me to have a photograph of himself.

If any such man exists he is a rare specimen and I want to preserve his picture for the museum, so all may see the man who "successfully" defied nature's laws. Successful men are not looking for short hours and easy jobs, for if they are truly successful they know that no such circumstance exists. Successful men are always looking for ways to lengthen instead of shorten the working days.

Hill: Have you always followed the habit of doing more than you were paid for, Mr. Carnegie?

Carnegie: If I had not done so you would not be here, seeking to learn the rules of successful achievement, for I would still be working as a day labourer, right where I began. If you asked me which of the principles of achievement has aided me most I think I would be compelled to say it was Going the Extra Mile. However, you must not reach the conclusion that this principle, alone can be depended upon for success. There are other success principles, some combination of which must be used by all who achieve outstanding and enduring success.

Now is an appropriate time to call your attention to the importance of combining Definiteness of Purpose with the habit of Going the Extra Mile. In going that extra mile one should have a definite, final destination in view, and I see no reason why one should not render more service than he is paid for as a deliberate means of influencing the wheel of life in the attainment of a definite goal.

What if one does follow this habit as a matter of expediency? It is every man's privilege to promote himself in every legitimate way possible, and especially it is his privilege to advance himself through methods which satisfy and benefit others.

The habit of rendering more than one is paid for is one habit against which no opposition can be legitimately offered. It is a habit which anyone may exercise on his own initiative, without the necessity of asking permission to do so. No purchaser of services will object if the seller delivers more than he promises. And surely no purchaser of services will object if the seller delivers the services with a friendly, pleasing mental attitude. These are privileges within the rights of the seller.

Hill: What about the man whose lack of education forces him to accept only such opportunities as are available to common labourers who work with their hands? Would you say that this man has an equal opportunity with those who have educated themselves?

Carnegie: I'm very glad you asked that question, because I want to set you right on a common mistake that people make in connection with this question of education.

First, let me explain that the word "educate" means something entirely different from that which many believe it to mean. The word has its roots in the Latin word educare, which means "to educe, to draw out, to develop from within." An educated man is one who has taken possession of his own mind and has so developed it, through organized thought, that it aids him efficiently in the solution of his daily problems in the business of living.

Some people believe that education consists of the acquisition of knowledge, but in a truer sense it means that one has learned how to use knowledge. I know many men who are walking encyclopedias of knowledge, but make such poor use of it that they cannot earn a living.

Another mistake that many people make is that of believing that schooling and education are synonymous terms. Schooling may enable a man to acquire much knowledge and assemble many useful facts, but schooling alone does not make a man educated. Education is self-acquired, and it comes through development and use of the mind, and in no other way.

Take Thomas A. Edison, for example. His entire schooling was a little more than three months, and it was not the most efficient of schooling at that. His real "schooling" came from the great School of Experience, from which he learned how to take possession of his own mind and to use it. Through this use he became one of the best educated men of our times. Such technical knowledge as he needed in the business of inventing he acquired from other men, through application of the Master Mind principle. In his work he requires knowledge of chemistry, physics, mathematics, and a great variety of other scientific subjects, none of which he personally understands. But since he is educated, he knows how and where to procure knowledge on these and all other subjects which are essential in his work.

So, disabuse your mind of the belief that knowledge, of itself, is education! The man who knows where and how to procure the knowledge he needs, when he needs it, is much more of a man of education than the man who has the knowledge but does not know what to do with it.

Now, there is another angle in connection with this old, time-worn alibi through which men explain away their failure by claiming they have had no opportunity to acquire education. It is the fact that schooling is free in this country, and it is so abundantly provided that any man can go to school at night if he really wishes to do so. We also have correspondence schools through which men may acquire knowledge on almost any subject, and for a very small price.

I have but little patience with those who claim that they have not succeeded because they lacked schooling, because I know that any man who really wants schooling can acquire it. The fallacy of this "no schooling" alibi, in most instances, is that it is used as an apology for plain laziness or lack of ambition.

I had but little schooling, and I began my career on exactly the same basis that any other working man begins. I had no "pull," no extra favours, no "rich uncle" to help me along, and no one to inspire me to promote myself into a more favourable economic status in life. The idea of doing so was entirely my own. Moreover, I found the task to be comparatively easy. It consisted, mainly, of my taking possession of my own mind and using it with Definiteness of Purpose. I did not like poverty, therefore I refused to remain under it. My own mental attitude on this subject was the determining factor that helped me to force poverty to give place to riches. I can truthfully tell you that of all the thousands of working men who have been employed by me, I do not know of one person who could not have equalled if not excelled me if he had wanted to do so.

Hill: Your analysis of the subject of education is both interesting and revealing, Mr. Carnegie, and you may rest assured I will include it in my writings on the philosophy of achievement, because I feel sure there are many others who have the wrong conception of the relationship between "schooling" and "education." If I understand you correctly, you believe the better part of one's education comes from doing and not merely from the acquisition of knowledge. Is that correct?

Carnegie: That is exactly correct! I have men working for me who have college degrees, but many of them find their college training only incidental to their success. Those who combine college training with practical experience soon become educated in a practical sense, provided they do not lean too heavily upon their academic degrees as a means of minimizing the importance of practical experience.

Right here is an appropriate place to tell you that the college graduates whom I have employed who develop the habit of rendering more service than they are paid for usually advance themselves to more responsible and better-paying positions very quickly, while those who neglect or refuse to adopt this principle make no more progress than the average man without college training.

Hill: Do you mean that college training is worth relatively less than the habit of doing more than one is paid for?

Carnegie: Yes, you might put it that way; but I have observed that men with college training who follow the habit of doing more than they are paid for, combining their college training with the advantages they gain from this habit, get ahead much more rapidly than men who do more than they are paid for but have no college training. From this I have reached the conclusion that there is a certain amount of thought discipline that a man gets from college training which men without this training do not generally possess.

Hill: Are the majority of the members of your Master Mind group men with college training, Mr. Carnegie?

Carnegie: No, about two-thirds of them are without college training, and I might add that the one who has been of greatest service to me, weighing everything they have all done, did not finish his common school training. It may be interesting, also, to know that his voluntary habit of rendering more service than he was paid for was the quality which made him of greatest value to me.

I say this because his example seemed to set the pace for other members of my Master Mind group. Moreover, his attitude on this subject spread to the rank and file of our workers, many of whom caught his spirit, practiced it, and thereby promoted themselves into better-paying and more responsible positions with the company.

Hill: Have you any definite method by which you endeavour to inform all your men of the advantages they may gain by rendering more service than they are paid for?

Carnegie: We have no direct method of doing this, although the news has been passed along, by the "grapevine" route, that the men who promote themselves to better positions follow the habit of doing more than they are paid for. I have often thought we should have gone much further by some form of more direct approach by which our men would have been taught the benefits of rendering this sort of service, and we would have done so had we not feared our efforts would have been misconstrued as an attempt on our part to get more work from our men without paying for it.

You see, most working men are skeptical and suspicious of all efforts on the part of an employer to influence them to improve themselves. Perhaps some smarter man than I will find a way through which employers may gain the confidence of their employees and convince them of the benefits, to employer and employee alike, of the habit of rendering more service than the wage scale calls for.

Of course, the rule must work both ways, and it will where an employee understands this principle and applies it deliberately. The matter is in the hands of the employee entirely. This is something he can do on his own initiative, without consulting the employer. The wiser employees discover and apply this principle voluntarily!

There is not a man in my Master Mind group who did not voluntarily promote himself to that position through the habit of doing more than was expected of him. I tell you frankly that the man who follows this habit voluntarily soon makes himself indispensable and thereby sets his own wages and chooses his own job. There is nothing an employer can do but cooperate with a man who has the sound judgment to do more than he is paid for.

Hill: But, Mr. Carnegie, aren't there some employers who selfishly refuse to recognize and reward an employee for the habit of doing more than he is paid for?

Carnegie: Undoubtedly, there are some employers who are short-sighted enough to withhold reward from a man of this type, but you must remember that the man who habitually does more than he is paid for is so rare, that there is keen competition among employers for his services.

If a man has the sound judgment to understand the advantages of doing more than he is paid for, he generally has sense enough, also, to know that all employers are seeking this sort of help; and even those who do not know this will, sooner or later, come to the attention of an employer who is looking for that sort of service, even though they do not deliberately endeavour to promote themselves.

Every man gravitates to where he belongs in life, just as surely as water seeks and finds its level!

Charlie Schwab, for example, did not seek me out (as far as I know) and say, "See here, I am doing more than I am paid for." I made the discovery in my own way because I was searching for that sort of mental attitude.

No employer can successfully conduct an industry of the size of ours without the aid of a large number of men who put heart, soul, and all the ability they have into their jobs. Therefore, I keep a close lookout at all times for this type of man, and when I find one I single him out for close observation, to make sure that he follows the habit consistently. The truth is that all successful employers do the same thing. That is one reason why they are successful.

Whether a man occupies the position of employer or employee, the space he occupies in the world is measured precisely by the quality and the quantity of the service he renders, plus the mental attitude in which he relates himself to other people. Emerson said, "Do the thing and you shall have the power." He never expressed a more truthful thought than this. Moreover, it applies to every calling, and to every human relationship. Men who gain and hold power do so by making themselves useful to others. All this talk about men holding fat jobs through "pull" is nonsense. A man may procure a good job through pull, but take my word for it when I tell you that if he remains in the job he will do so through "push," and the more of it he puts into the job the higher will he rise.

I have known of a few young men who were placed in positions beyond their earned merits and ability, through the influence of relatives or others, but seldom have I known of one of them making the fullest use of this unearned advantage; and such exceptions as I have known were due to their having acquired the habit of putting into their jobs more than they tried to take out.

Hill: What about the man who does not work for wages? The small merchant, or the doctor or lawyer? How can they promote themselves by rendering more service than they are paid for?

Carnegie: The rule applies to them the same as to the man who works for wages. As a matter of fact, those who fail to render such service remain small, and often they fail completely. There is a factor in a successful man's life known as "goodwill," without which no man can achieve noteworthy success in any calling.

The finest of all methods of building goodwill is that of rendering more service and better service than that which is expected. The man who does this, in the right sort of mental attitude, is sure to make friends who will continue to patronize him out of choice.

Moreover, his patrons will tell their friends about him, thereby putting the law of increasing returns into operation on his behalf.

The merchant may not be always in a position to put more merchandise in a package than the customer pays for, but he can wrap courteous service in the package and thereby build friendships that ensure him continuous patronage.

You see, goodwill and confidence are essentials of success in all walks of life. Without these one is forever confined to mediocrity. There is no better way of building these relationships than that of rendering more service and better service than that which is customary. This is one method of self-advancement which one may exercise on his own initiative, and generally speaking it is a form of service that can be rendered during odd time which would be otherwise wasted.

I have in mind a case that illustrates my point perfectly. Several years ago a policeman noticed a light burning at a late hour at night, in a small machine shop on his beat in which he knew no night work was done. Becoming suspicious, he telephoned the owner of the shop who came down immediately, unlocked the door and cautiously crept inside, with the policeman, gun in hand, at his side. When they reached the small room where the light appeared the owner of the shop looked in and, to his amazement, found one of his employees busily at work at a machine.

When you run out of something to do, try your hand at writing down a list of all the reasons why the world needs you. The experiment may surprise you.

The young man looked up, saw the employer and the policeman with a pistol pointed at him, then hurriedly explained that he had been in the habit of coming back to the shop at night so he could learn how to operate the machine and thereby make himself more useful to the employer.

I saw a small newspaper article concerning the circumstance, which claimed but three inches of space, one column, and described the event as something of a joke on the young man. But, to me, it was a joke on his employer. I sent for the young man to come to see me, talked with him a few minutes, and employed him at double the wages he was getting. Today he is the head of one of our most important plant operation departments, at a salary approximately four times as much as he was receiving when I found him.

But this is not the end of the story. This young man is on the way to still higher positions, and if he keeps on working with his present mental attitude he may fill the best job in the plant, or get into business for himself.

I tell you there is no way to hold down these fellows who spend their spare time preparing to render greater and better service. They go right on to the top of their profession or calling, as naturally as cork rises to the top in water.

I belong to a club, whose membership is made up of some two hundred men, a majority of whom have achieved success in their respective callings. A few weeks ago one of the members gave a banquet at which I was the guest speaker. It occurred to me to speak on the subject of the principles of individual achievement, so I had a list of these principles placed on each man's plate. In my talk I requested each man to place each of these principles in what he believed its relative position of importance to be, and to number each accordingly.

It was no surprise to me when I learned that more than two-thirds of those present placed the habit of doing more than is paid for at the head of the list.

Analyze any man who is an acknowledged success in his occupation and you will be likely to find that he follows the habit of doing more than is demanded of him, although in many instances he may be doing so unconsciously.

Hill: Mr. Carnegie, suppose that an employee renders more service and better service than he is paid for, but finds that his employer takes no cognizance of this sort of service? Should he go on rendering that sort of service without saying anything about increased pay, or would it be proper for him to bring the matter to the attention of his employer, with a direct request for the proper reward?

Carnegie: Every successful man is also an able salesman. Remember that! It is an individual's privilege to render more service than he is paid for, and it certainly is his duty to himself to market his services to best advantage. If he is doing more than he is paid for he has a sound reason for asking for increased compensation. As a matter of fact, he has no adequate reason for asking for more pay unless and until he can show that he is earning more than he is receiving.

I have seen many men ask for promotions, or increased pay, who did not have a single argument to support their requests. I remember a man coming into my office one day and asking for an increase of pay on the grounds that he had been working in the job he then held much longer than another man who was doing similar work, but receiving greater pay.

I replied to his demands by sending for the records of the two men from which it was obvious that the new man was turning out more work and better work than the one who had asked for increased pay. I wound up the interview by asking this man what he would do if he were in my place, and he replied that he would do just what he knew I was going to do—nothing.

However, not all men are as reasonable as this man was, under similar circumstances. There are many men who believe that priority in the matter of the period of their employment should entitle them to higher pay regardless of the quality and the quantity of service they render.

Obviously, the purchase and sale of personal services in trade and commerce is not unlike the purchase and sale of any commodity. The buyer cannot pay more than the value of that which he purchases and remain in business.

The law of supply and demand also enters into the bargain, and becomes a determining factor in the price of personal services, just the same as it does in connection with the purchase and sale of merchandise. The seller of personal services is in competition with others who have similar services for sale. When the saturation point in the market has been reached, the selling price naturally declines.

Hill: What can a man do when he finds himself in competition with others who are willing to work for less money than he desires or needs? How may an individual meet such competition?

Carnegie: He can meet it by delivering a better product than his competitor, and in no other way. All the king's horses and all the king's men cannot change this.

He can go still another long step forward in meeting competition by rendering service in the right sort of mental attitude. Beyond this there is only one thing a man can do to market personal services to better advantage and that is to specialize in some particular field in which competition is not so keen.

This may involve a change in his vocation, but it is a step I have known many ambitious men to take. If a man's work does not yield him enough to satisfy his needs, then the only thing he can do is to change into some other field, where the pay for services is higher.

In this connection, I wish to warn you of a common mistake made by men who work for wages. It is the all-too-common habit of confusing one's financial needs with one's demands for wages. I have known men whose habits were so extravagant, and whose home economics were so poorly managed, that they endeavoured to solve their problem of need for more money than they were making by demanding that it come in the form of higher wages, although they were already receiving the full value of their services.

On the whole, I think that both the employers and the employees in American industry are fair and reasonable. No sensible employer wants to purchase personal services for less than their value, and no fair-minded employee expects or demands pay out of proportion to the value of the services he renders; but there are some men on both sides who seem not to have a clear idea of how to arrive at a fair price for personal services.

Hill: In speaking of the relationship between employers and employees, I take it for granted, Mr. Carnegie, that you have reference to this relationship in its broadest meaning; that you refer to all circumstances under which personal services are purchased and sold such, for example, as the relationship between professional men and their clients, where the "wages" consist of a fixed fee; and the merchant and his patrons, where the "wages" consist of a profit on the merchandise sold.

Carnegie: Yes, you are correct; but you might have extended the scope of employer-employee relationship to include all relationships where one person renders service to another. The habit of doing more than one is expected to do can be applied very effectively in purely friendly relationships, where one person serves another without any thought of pecuniary gain. Here the object in rendering such service might be that of a desire to develop a more enduring friendship.

The principle may be applied effectively in family relationships, where the service rendered by one member of a family to other members comes under the classification of family duty. Here, as in all other relationships, it is beneficial to render more service and better service than is customary, and above all it pays to render the service in the right sort of mental attitude. Half the domestic disagreements in families could be overcome through a faithful application of the habit of doing more than is expected, and doing it in a pleasing spirit.

Hill: From what you have said, I have reached the conclusion that the habit of doing more than one is paid for has such broad possibilities of application that it may affect all human relationships.

Carnegie: Yes, it may serve beneficially in those relationships of mere acquaintanceship, where the question of service is not involved, and no obligation to render service exists. There are situations where the entire relationship consists of the mere exchange of pleasantries between strangers.

Right here I wish to emphasize the fact that the service one renders without pay, and without any expectation of direct compensation of a monetary nature, generally proves to be the most profitable service one can render, because such service builds friendships and places others under obligation in ways and to a degree that would be impossible if the service were paid for! Through the operation of the principles of retaliation and reciprocation all people express in some form their appreciation of the favours extended them, and as definitely show resentment of injuries done to them.

The favours may consist of nothing more tangible than mere words of courtesy, and the injuries may be no greater than the failure of a neglectful person to speak to an acquaintance whom he passes on the street, but the repercussions in both cases may be widespread and serious.

And I might carry the illustration a step further by saying that not only do mere words, or the lack of them, serve to alter relationships between people, but the tone of voice in which words are spoken may make either friends or enemies.

I know a very successful businessman who never speaks to one of his employees without carefully modifying his voice so as to make it carry a feeling of kindliness. For that matter he never speaks to anyone without controlling his voice so it will convey the feeling he desires it to convey.

This man not only injects pleasing tones into his voice when he speaks to his employees, but I have observed that when he gives an order he always does so by asking an employee if he will do thus and so, instead of demanding that he do it. The results of this, approach are astounding.

I have often wondered why people in all walks of life who wish to gain the friendly cooperation of others do not resort to this habit of asking for cooperation in a pleasant tone of voice instead of bluntly demanding it, as a majority of the people do.

Wouldn't it be better for all concerned if members of a family requested favours of one another, in a kindly tone of voice, instead of bluntly demanding attention? I have one neighbour who never gives an order to any of his children. If he desires one of them to do something he modifies the tone of his voice so that it carries a feeling of deep affection, and expresses his desires in the form of a question, Will you please do this or that? Or, Would your mind refraining from doing this or that?

The results are immediate and effective. His children respond in the same affectionate tone of voice, thereby signifying that it is a pleasure to comply with the request.

Here, then, is another illustration of how the principle of reciprocation works in practice. Whether in business, social, or family relationships, the habit of Going the Extra Mile pays handsomely. And it is surprising when one observes closely and discovers the great variety of human relationships in which one may go the extra mile with direct benefits.

Hill: Mr. Carnegie, you have given a very lucid description of the benefits available through the application of the habit of Going the

Extra Mile. Will you now give a brief summary of the most practical methods of developing this habit?

Carnegie: With this, as with all the other principles of the philosophy of achievement, perfection is attained only through practice. The word habit connotes repetition of a thought, word or deed. There is no other way to develop any habit.

To answer your question more specifically I would suggest that the best way to develop the habit of Going the Extra Mile is to adopt the policy of actually going the extra mile in all human relationships.

One might well begin at home, with the members of one's family. Most families need to practice this habit more.

Next, one might very profitably begin to go the extra mile on behalf of one's daily associates in business or vocational activity.

It might be very helpful, as a means of developing this habit, if not directly profitable otherwise, if one adopted the policy of Going the Extra Mile with chance acquaintances, through words and acts of courtesy. I have known of great opportunities for self-promotion to come from this sort of courtesy.

If you want something done, and done well, go to a busy man who so organizes his time that he has some to spare for emergencies.

Lastly, if one would adopt and deliberately follow the habit of Going the Extra Mile in all relationships with others, then there would be little chance of misunderstandings and practically no risk of loss of the opportunity for self-promotion.

One cannot overemphasize the importance of doing more than one is paid for as a matter of habit. It is not enough merely to do this for the sake of temporary expediency, when it is obvious that the act will bring benefits, for this leads to many an oversight of opportunities for self-promotion which can be uncovered only by those who are known to Go the Extra Mile as a matter of habit. This habit will attract and reveal opportunities that the average person would pass by unnoticed. Moreover, the habit has a strong tendency to create opportunities where none existed before.

All habits have the peculiarity of inspiring related habits. The habit of doing more than one is paid for will automatically aid in the development of the habits of initiative, perseverance, enthusiasm, imagination, self-control, definiteness of purpose, self-reliance, attractive personality, and many other qualities essential for success, among them a genuine affection for people.

You see, therefore, there are more benefits connected with the habit of doing more than one is paid for than those that are discernible by quick, surface analysis. I emphasize this fact because one may make the mistake of misjudging the importance of this habit because of the simplicity of its title. All of us should remember that the big things of life are nothing but an assembly of smaller things.

The difference between the acts that lead to success and those which lead to definite failure is often so slight that it is unnoticed by all except those who have a keenly discriminating sense of observation and analysis of the circumstances of human relationship.

Above all, we should remember that all success depends upon the manner with which one relates himself to others. Human relationship, therefore, is the most important subject of life. Here is where one becomes "the master of his fate, the captain of his soul," or goes down into the darkness of oblivion, through failure.

The tragedy of those who fail lies in the fact that human relationship is subject to manipulation, direction, influence and control, through established rules of success. If it were not so, there would be no purpose in presenting this philosophy of achievement.

In addition to all the other benefits available to those who habitually render more service and better service than they are paid for, this habit brings one a certain inner feeling of happiness which, of itself, would be adequate compensation for following the habit.

I have never known a person who followed this habit who did not reflect a disposition of optimism and cheerfulness! It would be well-nigh impossible for one to make it a part of his daily habits to render useful service to as many people as possible and at the same time express a grouchy, pessimistic mental attitude.

Another very effective method for the development of the habit of Going the Extra Mile is that of carefully analyzing and studying those who follow the habit and those who do not, and comparing the achievements of these two classes. One month of daily observation of people will be sufficient to convince one of the stupendous possibilities available to all who go the extra mile and go willingly and pleasantly.

Hill: I reach the conclusion that the term "Doing more than is paid for", is somewhat a misnomer in that it is impossible, in the broader meaning of this term, for one to do more than he is paid for. Is that your understanding, Mr. Carnegie?

Carnegie: I was waiting to see if you would grasp this point without my calling it to your attention! You are correct. All forms of constructive labour are rewarded, in one way or another, and in the broader sense there really is no such possibility as that of "Doing more than one is paid for."

Now let us see what specific benefits are available to man (through his exalted powers of thought and speech) which compensate him for Going the Extra Mile. The more useful of these compensating advantages are these:

Some Advantages of Doing More than One is Paid For:

1. The habit of Going the Extra Mile gives one the benefit of the Law of Increasing Returns, in a variety of ways too numerous to be described here.
2. This habit places one in a position to benefit by the Law of Compensation, through which no act or deed, will or can be expressed without an equivalent response (after its own nature).
3. It gives one the benefit of growth through resistance and use, thereby leading to mental development and increased skill in the use of the body. (It is a well-known fact that both body and mind attain efficiency and skill through systematic discipline and use which call for the rendering of service that temporarily is not paid for).
4. The habit develops the important factor of initiative, without which no individual ever rises above mediocrity in any calling.
5. It develops self-reliance, which is likewise an essential in all forms of personal achievement.
6. It enables an individual to profit by the law of contrast, since obviously a majority of the people do not follow the habit of doing more than they are paid for. On the contrary, they endeavour to "get by" with a minimum amount of service.
7. It helps one to defeat the habit of drifting aimlessly, thereby checking the habit which stands at the head of the major causes of failure.

8. It definitely aids in development of the habit of Definiteness of Purpose, which is the first principle of individual achievement.
9. It tends strongly to aid in the development of Attractiveness of Personality, thereby leading to the means by which one may relate himself to others so as to gain their friendly cooperation.
10. It often gives an individual a preferred position of relationship with others through which he may become indispensable, thereby fixing his own price on his services.
11. It ensures continuous employment, thereby serving as insurance against want in connection with the necessities of life.
12. It is the greatest of all the known methods by which the man who works for wages may promote himself to higher positions and better wages, and serves as a practical means by which a man may attain the position of ownership of a business or industry.
13. It develops alertness of the imagination, the faculty through which one may create practical plans for the attainment of one's aims and purposes in any calling.
14. It develops a positive "mental attitude", which is one of the more important qualities that are essential in all human relationships.
15. It serves to build the confidence of others in one's integrity and general ability, which is an indispensable essential for noteworthy achievement in every calling.
16. Finally, it is a habit which one may adopt and follow on his own initiative, without being under the necessity of asking the permission of anyone to do so.

Compare these sixteen definite advantages that are available to man, in return for doing more than he is paid for, with the one sole benefit of acquiring food necessary for existence that is available to the other creatures of the earth through the same habit, and you will be forced to the conclusion that overwhelmingly the greater number of benefits enjoyed by man serve as adequate compensation for his development and use of this habit. This comparison substantiates your statement that it is an impossibility for one to do more than one is paid for, and for the very obvious reason that in the mere act of doing that which is constructive one acquires power that can be converted into whatever one desires.

This analysis gives greater meaning to Emerson's statement, "Do the thing and you shall have the power."

No one who follows this analysis carefully can help discovering the truth that it is impossible for one to do more than one is paid for. The pay consists in the self-discipline and self-development one attains through the rendering of service, as well as in the material effects of the service, in the form of economic compensation.

Hill: Your analysis of the habit of doing more than one is paid for suggests that this habit is one of the "musts" of the philosophy of individual achievement. Will you describe some of the definite circumstances in your own business experience through which you have profited by the habit, Mr. Carnegie?

Carnegie: You have given me a big order. First, let me give you a blanket answer by saying that all the material riches I possess, and every business advantage I enjoy, might be attributable to my having followed this habit. But I will give you one specific example of an experience which gave me one of the greatest opportunities to promote myself that I ever enjoyed. I mention this particular experience because it was one of the most dramatic of my life, and I might add that it carried with it one of the greatest risks that I ever assumed in order to Go the Extra Mile. The risk was of that type which one should never assume unless he knows he is making the right move, and even then it is the sort of risk which might be fatal to one's opportunities for self-promotion under most circumstances.

It is more profitable to be for something than it is to be against something.

When I was a very young lad I studied telegraphy at night and learned to operate a telegraph key efficiently. (I was not paid to do this, nor did anyone tell me to do it). I was rewarded for my labour, however, by attracting the attention of Thomas Scott, division superintendent of the Pennsylvania Railroad, in Pittsburgh, who gave me the position as his private operator and clerk.

One morning I arrived at the office ahead of everyone else, and discovered that a bad train wreck had tied up the line and the whole division was in a jam.

The dispatcher was frantically calling Mr. Scott's office when I walked in, so I took the key and found out quickly what had happened. I tried to reach Mr. Scott by telephone, but his wife reported that he had left home. So, there I was, sitting on top of a veritable volcano that was sure to explode and ruin my chances with the Pennsylvania Railroad forever if I made the wrong move, and it might do the same thing if I made no move at all.

I knew precisely what my chief would have done had he been there, and also knew well enough what he might do to me if I assumed the risk of acting for him in such an important emergency.

But time was important, so I took the plunge and sent out to the train orders in his name that re-routed traffic and untied the traffic snarl.

When my chief arrived at the office he found a written report of what I had done, with my resignation attached to it, on his desk. I had violated one of the strictest rules of the railroad, so I made it easy for my chief to save face with his superiors by placing my own head on the block.

About two hours later I received the verdict. My resignation came back to me with the words "Resignation refused" boldly written across it in the chief's handwriting. He made no further reference to the circumstance until several days later, and even then he brought the subject up, discussed it in his own way, and dismissed it without either reprimanding me or giving me a clean bill of health for my violation of the rules. He simply said: "There are two types of men who never get far in life. One is the type that cannot do what he is told, and the other is the type that can do nothing else." Here the subject was dismissed with an air of finality which enabled me to determine that he did not place me in either group.

It should be the aim of every young man to go beyond the sphere of his immediate instructions and render service that is not required of him, but one should be extremely cautious in assuming such risks beyond the letter of his instructions as I did on this occasion. Above all, he must know that he is making the right move, but even then he may at times run into difficulty.

A young man who worked as confidential secretary to a New York broker lost his job by mixing bad judgment with his well-meant exercise of the habit of going beyond the letter of his instructions. His chief went away for a vacation and left him in-charge of certain funds which he was to invest in the stock market, at a definite time and in a definite manner. Instead of following his instructions, he invested the funds in an entirely different manner. The transaction yielded a much greater profit than would have been received had the employer's instructions been carried out, but the employer took the view that the young man's violation of specific instructions clearly marked him as one who lacked sound judgment, and reasoned that he might violate his instructions again some time, under circumstances that would be disastrous. The result was a discharge.

So, I repeat, with emphasis, be sure you are right before breaking rules in order to do more than you are paid for, and be sure of your relationship with the man who may swing the axe above your neck for doing so. There is no quality that can take the place of sound, well-balanced judgment. Be active, be persistent, be definite, but also be cautious in your judgment.

Hill: Mr. Carnegie, would you mind explaining what benefits you received from having taken so great a risk as you did by breaking a strict rule of the railroad in order to do more than you were authorized to do? Would you say that the benefits you received justified the risk you assumed?

Carnegie: I can best answer your questions by saying that the move I made brought me to the attention of men outside of the railroad officials under whom I worked, who afterward supplied the money I needed to get started in the steel business. The very daring step I took gave me an opportunity to attract attention where it was of greatest help to me, although of course I did not have this in mind when I exceeded my authority and cleared the traffic jam.

The circumstance not only attracted attention to me, but it gave me a chance to prove that I had the courage to break rules when they should have been broken. It also established my ability to use sound judgment. If my judgment had been unsound the move I made would have had the effect of ruining my immediate chance to attract the favourable attention of men who were in a position to be of great help to me, and of course it would have meant my discharge by the railroad company.

Many years after this incident, when I invited a group of men to join me in supplying the capital for my first steel plant, Thomas Scott was the man who convinced the others that their money would be wisely invested in my enterprise. He referred to the circumstance of the railroad wreck as evidence that I had ability to deal with business emergencies in a dependable manner.

If I had to deal with the same emergency again I would handle it exactly as I did. The man who cannot deal with emergencies with sound judgment never can become indispensable in any business, as business cannot be operated successfully on unbreakable rules. The rub comes in knowing when to break them.

Hill: Mr. Carnegie, is it your policy always to encourage your employees to use their own judgment when they go beyond the letter of their instructions in applying the principle of doing more than they are paid for?

Carnegie: Every person associated with me, in any capacity, knows that he has the privilege of using his own initiative wherever he is willing to back it with his own judgment, and I encourage all my associates to do this, but I also go out of my way to emphasize, by example, the importance of using sound judgment where one exceeds his specific instructions. Up to the point where a man moves entirely on his specific instructions I back him, whether he succeeds or fails, but beyond that point, where a man moves on his own judgment he must assume the responsibility of his mistakes. Any other policy would be ruinous, both to an employer and an employee, because it would invite carelessness.

Hill: Are there any circumstances which you can recall, Mr. Carnegie, under which the habit of doing more than one is paid for would be inadvisable or harmful to anyone?

Carnegie: Let me answer your question by asking one: How could any habit which benefits both the purchaser and the seller of personal services harm anyone? In this transaction, there are only two parties. Therefore, no circumstance in connection with the habit of doing more than one is paid for that I can think of would be objectionable, to either the buyer or the seller, or to any outside person.

Hill: Let me put the question in another way, then, by asking which of the parties, the buyer or the seller of personal services rendered under the habit of delivering more than is paid for, is apt to get the better part of the bargain?

Carnegie: Generally speaking, I would say that there is no "better part" of any bargain which satisfies all parties to the transaction. However, in this particular instance I think you see that the seller gets the better part of the bargain. I have given you a description of sixteen definite benefits that accrue to the advantage of the seller of services under this policy, while it is obvious that the advantages to the purchaser from the same transaction are fewer by far.

When you consider the fact that the habit of doing more than is paid for is the most dependable of all methods of self-promotion through which an ordinary workman may raise himself to a position of economic security, I think you will need no further evidence that this habit should be of greater concern to an employee than it is to an employer.

Hill: Would you say that you could have achieved the success you have attained if you had refused to deliver more service than you were paid for? Is there any other policy that you could have substituted for that of doing more than you were paid for which would have served the same end?

Carnegie: There is no substitute for the habit of Going the Extra Mile, although some very smart men have tried, without satisfactory results, to achieve success without observing this rule. It would have been utterly impossible for me to have promoted my own interests, as I have done, if I had not formed the habit, early in life, of doing more than was expected of me.

Hill: I take it then, from your statement, that you consider the habit of doing more than one is paid for to have been more beneficial to you than the Master Mind principle to which you have paid a high tribute as a contributory influence in your business?

Carnegie: Yes, that is true, and I might add that if I had not followed the habit of doing more than I was paid for, I probably would never have reached the point at which a Master Mind alliance would have been of any benefit to me.

If you recall what I have said about my relationship with the members of my Master Mind group, you will see that the benefits I received from my associates were due, in a large measure, to my having arranged for each of them to earn more than he probably could have earned without my help.

You must remember that the habit of Going the Extra Mile is a privilege that is as available and as profitable to an employer, in some respects, as it is to an employee. From an employer's viewpoint, the habit of paying for more services than he actually receives, if he does it under the right sort of an understanding, often has the effect of enabling him not only to get, eventually, all that he pays for, but he may receive an overplus of great value in the form of loyalty and dependability.

Hill: That is exactly the point I wished to bring out. From your analysis one is left no alternative but to conclude that both the employer and the employee may profit by dealing with one another on the basis of delivering more than is paid for. Endeavouring to determine which receives the better part of the bargain, under such a policy, the employer or the employee, is something like trying to decide which comes first, the hen or the egg.

Carnegie: Your analysis is quite correct. Analyse this policy from any angle you wish and you will come, finally, to recognize that it is beneficial to all whom it affects, whether it be the employer or the employee. And you might well go a step further and say that the policy also benefits in a majority of the cases the public which is served by both employer and employee. The one element you cannot find, in connection with this policy, is any circumstance whereby anyone is injured.

On the other hand, I can easily name a long list of circumstances under which both the employer and the employee, as well as the public they serve, are irreparably injured by failure to observe this policy. I will not mention these circumstances because they are so obvious and well known that to describe them would be a waste of time. It might also trample on the toes of those who like to attribute their failure to get ahead in life to greedy employers who refuse to pay them what they think they are worth.

You know of course that most men who do not get ahead make the mistake of looking everywhere except in a mirror for the cause of their misfortune. This is one trait of human nature for which I refuse to suggest any remedy, and for the very good reason that the remedy would not be accepted if it were offered to such men.

I have always claimed that no man of sound mind and body, who is a citizen of our country, has any legitimate right to charge others with his failure to get ahead. Under our form of democracy, every man has the privilege of promoting himself into whatever position in life he is capable of filling, and you may be sure that most of the complaints about lack of opportunity are nothing but thin alibis with which people try to explain away indifference, lack of ambition or outright laziness.

I speak from both personal experience and observation when I say that American opportunities are so abundant and American resources are so great that the humblest person, with a sound body and a sound mind, can attain economic security. And I could name many men who have attained independence without a sound body.

Hill: What about the man who belongs to a trade union and is forced, by the rules of his union, to limit the quantity of work he performs? What chance has he to profit by the habit of doing more than he is paid for?

Carnegie: I knew you would be getting around to that question sooner or later. Now that you have asked it, let me deal with the question fairly and frankly, because I may as well tell you now my view on this subject.

In the first place, I wish to preface my remarks with the statement that I believe working men have the same right to organize for co-operative bargaining that any other group has. On this point there can be no room for argument. But the mere fact that men pool their power, whether it is for collective bargaining in connection with the sale of their personal services or the marketing of commodities, does not provide them with the right or the power to ignore the principles of economics or the public welfare.

No one can take out of any transaction more than has been put into it in equivalent values. That is an acknowledged rule of economics.

Very well, let me answer your question by saying that the man who allies himself with others under rules which force him to limit the quantity of service he renders in proportion to his remuneration thereby places himself in a position where he is forced to accept limited compensation. He may be able to command the top of the wage scale fixed by his union, but there he must stop. No union alliance can take him one step further and no union leader can assure him anything more.

The question then becomes one of determining whether or not an individual is willing to limit his style of living to fit the limited pay his union rules force upon him. That is something every man must decide for himself.

Hill: Judging by your business achievements, I assume that you chose to take your chances without the protection of a trade union, because you desired greater compensation than you could command through such an alliance. Is that correct?

Carnegie: That states my case exactly. I was approached many times by fellow workmen who invited me to join trade unions, but I declined, and for the very sound reason that I preferred to market my services in the open market where I could take advantage of a greater portion of the American opportunity to accumulate wealth than would have been available to me through the limited protection of a trade union. I had the right to make this choice. The American form of government was founded with that right as one of its major foundation stones, and I think it is this very privilege which, more than all others, makes this the greatest country in the world.

Where, except in this country, can a man start at scratch, without working capital, without great influence, and exchange his personal services for whatever amount of wealth he is capable of earning?

Hill: What would happen, Mr. Carnegie, if all men were forced, by law, to buy and sell personal services under trade union rules which limit the quantity of service any man can perform? Would that be a help or a hindrance to the majority of the people?

Carnegie: If that happened we would no longer have the right of free enterprise. It would have its repercussions in many other forms of curtailment of personal liberty, and very soon American freedom and liberty would be nothing but an empty phrase. I do not believe the American people would welcome anything that would curtail their privilege of self-determination because they have established a standard of living they could not maintain under such a curtailment.

Hill: But, Mr. Carnegie, wouldn't it help the poor and the weak if wage scales and working hours were established by law? Wouldn't such a law have the effect of distributing the wealth of America more evenly?

Carnegie: I will answer your questions in the light of what I have learned about laws and people from personal observation and practical business experience. In the first place, let us be perfectly frank in answering this question concerning the poor and the weak.

If you will observe nature's plan carefully you will see that nature does not protect the weak. She kills off the weak and encourages the strong in every species of living things, from the smallest insect to man himself. The law of survival of the fittest is so well recognized that it needs no further proof of its existence.

The greatest help that anyone can extend to the weak and the poor is that which enables them to help themselves. I had this very fact in mind when I told you I intended to distribute the better portion of my riches to the people, through the philosophy of individual achievement, because I knew that material wealth gravitates to the man who has the knowledge with which wealth is accumulated, just as definitely as water seeks its level.

This fact was well demonstrated during the War Between the States when the government gave a group of prisoners the privilege of gaining their freedom on the condition that they join the Union Army and go West and help put down Indian skirmishes. Many of them accepted, the condition being that inasmuch as they would be away for a long while they were to receive several months' pay in advance. The army started on its way, and I was informed by one of the soldiers in charge that by the end of the first week out every dollar of that advance pay was in the hands of fewer than half a dozen men who were clever with cards.

The same thing would occur if every dollar in America were placed in a pool and the entire amount were divided equally between the people. In a very short time the money would be back into the hands of those who are money-conscious—those who have the knowledge with which money is accumulated.

Now this is human nature of which I am speaking. All this talk about helping the weak and the poor by giving them something for nothing comes from men who have no practical understanding of how this can be done. I believe in helping the weak and the poor. I wouldn't be quite human if I didn't. Yet I know that the only way to permanently help anyone is to help him solve his problems through his own efforts.

Moreover, I have learned from experience that this is all the help a real man desires. Only the professional beggar and the indolent who are too lazy to work for a living would ask others to give them something for nothing. This class we will have with us always, but there is no charity in giving to those who will not try to help themselves.

Hill: You believe, then, that the best way to distribute the wealth of America is by providing all who will use it with the knowledge through which wealth is earned?

Carnegie: That is the only safe way. And there is another fact in connection with the term "wealth" to which I wish to call attention. It is the fact that the "American wealth" of which you speak consists of a combination of intelligently applied knowledge and the material resources of the nation. The material resources were here while the Indians owned the country, but it was worth nothing until men of practical education took it over and gave it bankable values by mixing knowledge with it.

Now this is my idea of helping the weak and the poor!

And here is something else I wish to mention in connection with this sort of help: It is a form of riches which cannot be lost, stolen or dissipated through unwise use. The wealth represented by knowledge and experience is perpetual. No bank failure can diminish it. No panic can destroy it. No wastrel can inherit it and destroy himself through its unwise use, as inherited money is often the means of self-destruction.

The giving of money often does more harm than good. The giving of knowledge never does harm, but it may ensure one against many forms of injury. If you doubt this, study carefully what happens to many who are born to a legacy of money which they did not earn.

There is still another point about the earning of money I wish to emphasize. It is the fact that it can become, and that it generally does become, a fascinating game through which one develops the pride of achievement. It also develops creative ability and adds to the national wealth in the form of able leadership which may be of great benefit in times of national emergencies.

Hill: Then you believe in the spirit of pioneering through which men take chances on their own initiative?

Carnegie: I have a sound reason for believing in it. If there had been no such spirit in America we would have none of the great industrial enterprises through which our natural resources have been developed.

It was the spirit of the pioneer which inspired James J. Hill to marry the East to the West, through the Great Northern Railroad.

It was the spirit of the pioneer which urged Thomas A. Edison on through ten thousand failures, until he triumphed, at last, in perfecting the incandescent electric lamp and a hundred other useful inventions which have added hundreds of millions of dollars of wealth to the country, to say nothing of providing employment for thousands of men and women.

It was the spirit of the pioneer which gave America the great Wanamaker store and the Marshall Field store.

It was the spirit of the pioneer which gave America her birth of liberty and freedom. All these leaders were urged on by the spirit of the pioneer which asks for no subsidies and recognizes no such thing as something for nothing.

Every great business and every industry in America owes its birth to the pioneering spirit of some man or group of men who asked nothing except the privilege of exercising their American rights of liberty and freedom through which they moved on their own initiative. These men made no demands in the name of the weak and the poor, although most of them were exceedingly poor at the outset.

I know a great deal about the weak and the poor. I was poor when I came to this country, but I was not weak. My strength consisted in my will to win by rendering useful service in return for the material riches I desired.

I am thankful that no misguided person coddled me because I was "a poor immigrant boy." If anyone had done so I might have been misled into believing, as some others are, that this country owed me a living.

Because I was not weak I recognized that this country owed me nothing except that which is the privilege of every citizen, and that is the right to render useful service and collect an equivalent return in the form of riches.

Hill: If I follow your analysis clearly, Mr. Carnegie, it is your belief that any gift which places in one's hands something of value which has not been earned may do that person an injury by destroying his incentive to render service. Is that your belief?

Carnegie: Yes, that is my belief, and I acquired it from a lifetime of practical experience in dealing with many thousands of men. A man's greatest asset is his desire to create, on his own initiative. There is no thrill like that which a man experiences when he begins to acquire economic freedom through his own efforts. Riches acquired in this manner not only give their owner more pleasure than those which come without effort, but they are more easily retained, for it generally follows that the man who learns how to acquire wealth learns at the same time how to use it and how to keep it.

Parents who are wealthy often condemn their children to eternal penury and failure by removing from them the necessity of rendering useful service. We have a case of that sort right here in Pittsburgh, a the present time. A young man named Harry Thaw inherited an income of $85,000 a year, right after leaving college. Instead of going to work and making himself useful he went to New York City and began to dazzle Broadway with his unearned riches. Very soon his debauchery led to his murdering a prominent architect, and now he is in prison for life, having barely escaped a worse fate.

I regret to say I do not place the blame for his sad plight on the young man. The real offender was the one who condemned the young man to a life of idleness and dissipation, by depriving him of the privilege of working, through a gift of money he did not earn.

Hill: Do you mean that the principle of Going the Extra Mile should not be applied between parents and their children?

Carnegie: Oh, no! I don't mean that. Parents owe their children a gift, but it should be a gift of education and preparation for life, and not a gift of money. Money is never a greater curse than when it is lavished on children by their parents, for purposes other than those of preparing them to become self-determining.

Hill: From your own experience can you say that great wealth brings happiness?

Carnegie: Nothing brings enduring happiness except some form of useful service. Understand this truth and you will have the soundest of all reasons for rendering more service and better service than you are paid for directly. The man who goes the extra mile brings back with him a feeling of satisfaction he can get in no other way. This is one form of compensation which, alone, is sufficient justification for doing more than one is paid for. It is a compensation which cannot be withheld; a form of riches of which one cannot be deprived.

Hill: Why do so few people make use of the principle of Going the Extra Mile?

Carnegie: Because so few have been taught the benefits this habit will yield. The place to begin teaching this principle is in the home. Every child should be taught that it is profitable to render useful service for which it receives no immediate pay other than the satisfaction that comes from the service. But the teaching should go beyond this point and clearly show the child that this habit can become a great asset throughout life. Similar training should be a part of every public school curriculum, so that by the time boys and girls reach high school they will observe and apply this principle as definitely as they perform any other duty connected with their studies.

Here, as in most other instances where training of children is neglected, we adults are to blame for their lack of knowledge. Children are the victims of older people who are responsible for their guidance. Neglect in such important matters as that of failing to teach them the benefits of Going the Extra Mile is very little short of a criminal act.

Analysis of chapter three: Going the extra mile

by Napoleon Hill

Nature has so arranged the universe that there is no such reality as something for nothing. Everything has its price, or its equivalent in something else. Sometimes men unwisely spend their time trying to invent machines of perpetual motion which they hope will enable them to circumvent the laws of motion. All of them have ended in severe disappointment.

Other men just as unwisely try to collect a full day's pay for a poor day's labour. By force of numbers they may ally themselves in groups and succeed, for a time; but sooner than is convenient for them they pay for their folly by the loss of the market for their services. Nature cannot be successfully defied, although some men never seem to learn this truth.

In this chapter, Mr. Carnegie has presented an understandable description of several principles of human conduct, as they apply in the ordinary daily relationships of men. His description has been frank and definite. Coming, as it has, from one of America's recognized leaders in industry, his analysis is unavoidably impressive.

The most important test of these principles will be that which an individual gives them by applying them in his own personal relationships with others. The test will be more beneficial if one makes it deliberately with a definite purpose in mind.

Fortunately, the author had the rare privileges of observation of those who have risen to great heights of achievement as well as those who have gone down in defeat. Some twenty years ago the editor of *The Golden Rule Magazine* was invited to deliver a speech at the Palmer School in Davenport, Iowa. He accepted the invitation on his regular fee basis, which was $100 and travelling expenses.

While the editor was at the college he picked up enough editorial material for several stories for his magazine. After he had delivered the speech and was ready to return to Chicago, he was asked by Dr. B.J. Palmer to turn in his expense account and receive his pay. He declined to accept any money for either his address or his expenses, explaining that he had already been paid adequately by the material he had procured for his magazine. He took the train and went back to Chicago, feeling well repaid for his trip.

The following week he began to receive from Davenport many subscriptions to his magazine. By the end of the week he had received over $6,000 in cash subscriptions. Then followed a letter from Dr. Palmer, explaining that the subscriptions had come from his students, who had been told of the editor's refusal to accept money he had been promised and had earned.

During the following two years, the students and graduates of the Palmer School sent in more than $50,000 in subscriptions to *The Golden Rule Magazine*. The story was so impressive that it was written up in a magazine that had a circulation throughout the English-speaking world, and then subscriptions came from many different countries.

Thus, by rendering $100 worth of service without collecting for it, the editor had started the law of Increasing Returns to work in his behalf, and it yielded him a return of over 500% on his investment. Going the Extra Mile is no pipe-dream. It pays off and pays off handsomely!

Moreover, it never forgets! Like other types of investment, the habit of Going the Extra Mile often yields dividends throughout one's lifetime.

Let's look at what may happen when one neglects an opportunity to Go the Extra Mile. Late one rainy afternoon an automobile salesman sat at his desk, in the showroom of the New York branch office. The door opened and in walked a man jauntily swinging a cane.

The salesman looked up from the reading of the afternoon paper, took a swift glance at the newcomer, and immediately spotted him as another of those Broadway "window shoppers" who do nothing but waste one's valuable time. He went ahead with his newspaper, not taking the trouble to get up from his seat.

The man with the cane walked through the showroom, looking at first one car and then another. Finally, he walked over to where the salesman was sitting, teetered himself on his cane, and nonchalantly asked the price of three different automobiles he had seen. Without looking up from his newspaper, the salesman gave the prices and went on with his reading.

The man with the cane walked back over to the three automobiles at which he had been looking, kicked the tires of each one, then walked back to the busy man at the desk and said, "Well, I hardly know whether I shall take this one, or that one over there; or whether I shall just buy all three."

The busy man at the desk responded with a sort of smirky, wiseacre smile, as much as to say, "Just as I thought!"

Then the man with the cane said, "Oh, I guess I will only buy one of them. Send that one with the yellow wheels up to my house tomorrow. And, by the way, how much did you say it was?"

He took out his cheque book and wrote out a cheque, handed it to the salesman, and walked out. When the salesman saw the name on the cheque, he turned pink and nearly fainted. The man who signed the check was Charles Payne Whitney, and the salesman knew then, as well as he knew his own name, that if he had only taken the time to get up from his seat he might have sold all three automobiles without any great effort.

When the management heard of the incident, the salesman was fired on the spot! The punishment was mild. He probably should have been forced to pay for the loss of profits on the two cars he did not sell. Withholding anything short of the best service of which one is capable is costly business, a fact which many have learned after it was too late. The right of personal initiative is not worth much to the fellow who is too indifferent or too lazy to exercise it. Many people are in this class without recognizing the reason why they never accumulate riches.

Over forty years ago, a young salesman in a hardware store observed that the store had a lot of odds and ends which were out of date and were not selling. Having time on his hands, he rigged up a special table in the middle of the store. He loaded it with some of the unsalable merchandise, marking it at the bargain price of a dime an article. To his surprise and that of the owner of the store, the gadgets sold readily.

Out of that experience grew the great F.W. Woolworth Five and Ten Cent chain store system. The young man who stumbled upon the idea by Going the Extra Mile was Frank W. Woolworth.

Before he died, the idea yielded him a fortune estimated at more than $50,000,000. Moreover, the same idea made several other persons rich, and applications of the idea are at the heart of many more profitable merchandising systems of America.

No one told young Woolworth to exercise his right to personal initiative. No one paid him for doing so; yet his action led to ever-increasing returns for his efforts. Once he put the idea into practice, increasing returns nearly ran him down.

There is something about this habit of doing more than one is paid for which works in one's behalf even while one sleeps. Once it begins to work, it piles up riches so fast that it seems like some queer sort of magic which, like Aladdin's Lamp, draws to one's aid an army of genii which come laden with bags of gold.

The habit of Going the Extra Mile is one that does not confine its rewards to wage earners. It works as well for an employer as it does for an employee, as one merchant whom I knew quite well has gratefully testified.

His name was Arthur Nash, and his business was that of a merchant tailor. Some twenty-odd years ago Mr. Nash found his business just one step ahead of the sheriff. The First World War and other conditions over which he seemed to have no control had brought him to the brink of financial ruin. One of his most serious handicaps was that his employees caught his spirit of defeatism and expressed it in their work by slowing down and becoming disgruntled. His situation was desperate. Something had to be done and it had to be done quickly if he was to continue in business.

Out of sheer desperation he called his employees together and told them of the condition he was in. While he was speaking, an idea occurred to him. He said he had been reading a story in *The Golden Rule Magazine* which told how its editor had Gone the Extra Mile by rendering service for which he refused to accept any pay, only to be voluntarily rewarded with more than $6,000 worth of subscriptions to his magazine. He wound up by suggesting that if he and all his employees caught the spirit and began to Go the Extra Mile they might save the business. He promised his employees that if they would join with him in an experiment he would endeavour to carry on the business, with the understanding that everyone would forget wages, forget working hours, pitch in and do his best, and take chances on receiving pay for his work. If the business could be made to pay, every employee would receive his back wages, with a bonus thrown in for good measure.

The employees liked the idea and agreed to give it a trial. The next day they began to come in with their meager savings which they voluntarily loaned to Mr. Nash. Everyone went to work with a new spirit, and the business began to show signs of new life. Very soon it was back on a paying basis. Then it began to prosper as it had never prospered before. Ten years later the business had made Mr. Nash richer than he needed to be. The employees were more prosperous than they had ever been, and everyone was happy.

Arthur Nash has passed on, but today the business continues as one of the more successful merchant tailoring businesses of America. The employees took over the business when Mr. Nash laid it down. Ask any one of them what he thinks of this business of Going the Extra Mile, and you will get the answer in a hurry! Moreover, talk with one of the Nash salesmen, wherever you meet one, and observe his spirit of enthusiasm and self-reliance. When this "extra-mile" stimulant gets into a man's mind, he becomes a different sort of person. The outlook on the world appears different to him, and he appears different because he is different!

Here is the right place to remind you of an important thing about the habit of Going the Extra Mile by doing more than one is paid for. It is the strange influence it has on the man who does it. The greatest benefit from this habit does not come from those to whom the service is rendered. It comes from the one who renders the service in the form of a changed "mental attitude" which gives him more influence with other people, more self-reliance, greater initiative, enthusiasm, vision and definiteness of purpose; all of these are qualities of successful achievement.

"Do the thing and you shall have the power," said Emerson. Ah yes, the power! What can a man do in our world without power? But it must be the sort of power that attracts other people instead of repelling them. It must be a form of power which gains momentum from natural law, through the operation of which one's acts and deeds come back to him greatly multiplied.

To benefit by the habit of doing more than one is paid for, one should understand the meaning back of the Biblical quotation, "Whatsoever a man soweth that shall he also reap." The sort of seed a man sows is important! It is important because every seed of service one sows brings back a crop after its own kind.

You who work for wages should learn more about this sowing and reaping business. Then you would understand why no man can go on forever sowing the seed of inadequate service and reaping a harvest of full-grown pay. You would know that there must come a halt to the habit of demanding a full day's pay for a poor day's work.

By force men may, for a time, squeeze more blood out of a turnip than nature placed in it, but nature is too resourceful to tolerate such a violation of her plans for long. Sooner or later she strikes back with a terrible vengeance at those who either ignorantly or willfully run counter to her plans.

And you who do not work for wages but wish to get more of the better things of life. Let me have a word with you, too. Why don't you turn smart and start getting what you want the easy and sure way? Yes, there is an easy and sure way to promote one's self into whatever he wants from life, and its secret becomes known to every person who makes it his business to Go the Extra Mile. The secret can be uncovered in no other manner, for it is wrapped up in that extra mile.

The pot of gold at the "end of the rainbow" is no mere fairy tale! The end of that extra mile is the spot where the rainbow ends, and there is where the pot of gold is hidden.

Few people ever catch up with the end of the rainbow. When one gets to where he thought the rainbow ended, he finds it is still far in the distance. The trouble with most of us is that we do not know how to follow rainbows. Those who know the secret know that the rainbow really can be reached only by Going the Extra Mile.

Late one afternoon, some twenty-five years ago, William C. Durant, the founder of General Motors, walked into his bank after banking hours, and asked for some favour which, in the ordinary course of business, should have been requested during banking hours.

The man who granted the favour was Carrol Downes, an under-official of the bank. He not only served Mr. Durant with efficiency, but he went the Extra Mile and added courtesy to the service. He made Mr. Durant feel that it was a real pleasure to serve him. The incident seemed trivial, and of itself it was of very little importance. Unknown to Mr. Downes, this courtesy was destined to have repercussions of a far-reaching nature.

The next day Mr. Durant asked Mr. Downes to come to see him at his office. That visit led to the offer of a position which Downes accepted. He was given a desk in a general office where nearly a hundred other people worked, and notified that the office hours were from 8:30 a.m. to 5:30 p.m. His salary to begin with was modest.

At the end of the first day, when the gong rang, announcing the close of the day's work, Downes noticed that everyone grabbed his hat and coat and made a rush for the door. He sat still, waiting for the others to get out. After they had gone he remained at his desk, pondering in his own mind the cause of the great haste everyone had shown to get away on the very second of quitting time. Fifteen minutes later Mr. Durant opened the door of his private office, saw Downes still at his desk, and asked if he hadn't understood that he was privileged to quit work at 5:30.

"Oh yes," Downes replied, "but I didn't wish to be run over in the rush." Then he asked if he could be of any service to Mr. Durant.

He was told that he might find a pencil for the motor magnate. He got the pencil, ran it through the pencil sharpener, then took it in. Mr. Durant thanked him and said good night.

The next day at quitting time Downes remained at his desk again, after the "rush" was over. This time he waited with purpose aforethought. In a little-while Mr. Durant came out of his private office and asked, again, if Downes didn't understand that 5:30 was quitting time.

"Yes," Downes smiled, "I understand it is quitting time for the others, but I have heard no one say that I have to leave the office when the day is officially closed, so I chose to remain here with the hope that I might be of some slight service to you."

"What an unusual hope!" Durant exclaimed. "Where did you get the idea?"

"I got it from the scene I witness here at closing time every day," Downes replied. Mr. Durant grunted some reply which Downes didn't hear clearly, and went back into his office.

From then on Downes perched himself at his desk at quitting time, and remained there until he saw Mr. Durant put on his hat and coat and leave for the day. He was not paid to remain over time. No one told him to do it. No one promised him anything for remaining, and as far as the casual observer might know, he was wasting his time.

Several months later Downes was called into Mr. Durant's office and informed that he had been chosen to go out to a new plant that had been recently purchased, to supervise the installation of the plant machinery. Imagine that! A former bank official becoming a machinery expert in a few months.

Without quibbling, Downes accepted the assignment and went on his way. He didn't say, "Why, Mr. Durant, I know nothing about the installation of machinery." He didn't say, "That's not my job," or "I'm not paid to install machinery." No, he went to work and did what was requested of him. Moreover, he went at the job with a pleasant "mental attitude."

Three months later the job was completed. It was done so well that Mr. Durant called Downes into his office and asked him where he learned about machinery. "Oh," Downes explained, "I never learned, Mr. Durant. I merely looked around, found men who knew how to get the job done, put them to work, and they did it."

"Splendid!" Durant shouted. "There are two types of men who are valuable. One is the fellow who can do something and do it well, without complaining that he is being overworked. The other is the fellow who can get other people to do things well, without complaining. You are both types wrapped into one package."

Downes thanked him for the compliment and turned to go. "Wait a moment," Durant requested. "I forgot to tell you that you are the new manager of the plant you have installed, and your salary to start with is $50,000 a year!"

The following ten years of association with Durant were worth between ten and twelve million dollars to Carroll Downes. He became an intimate advisor of the motor king and made himself rich for his pains.

The main trouble with so many of us is that we see men who have arrived and weigh them in the hour of their triumph without taking the pains to find out how or why they "arrived."

There is nothing very dramatic about the story of Carroll Downes. The incidents mentioned occurred in the day's business, without even passing notice by the average person who worked along with Downes. And I doubt not that many of these fellow workers envied him because they believed he had been favoured by Durant, through some sort of pull or luck or whatever it is that men who do not succeed use as an excuse to explain their failure.

Well, to be candid, Downes did have an inside "pull" with Durant! He created that "pull" on his own initiative. He created it by Going the Extra Mile in as trivial a matter as that of placing a neat point on a pencil when nothing was requested except a plain pencil. He created it by remaining at his desk "with the hope" that he might be of service to Durant after the "rush" was over at 5:30 each evening. He created it by using his right of personal initiative by finding men who understood how to install machinery instead of asking Durant where or how to find such men.

Trace down this incident, step by step, and you will find that Downes' success was due solely to his own initiative. Moreover, it consists of a series of little tasks well performed, in the right "mental attitude."

Perhaps there were a hundred other men working for Durant who could have done as well as Downes, but the trouble with them was that they were searching for the end of the rainbow by running away from it in the 5:30 rush each afternoon.

Long years after this incident, this writer asked Carroll Downes how he got his opportunity with Mr. Durant. "Oh," he modestly replied, "I just made it my business to get in his way, so he could see me. When he looked around, wanting some little service, he called on me because I was the only one in sight. In time he got into the habit of calling on me."

There you have it! Mr. Durant "got into the habit", of calling on Downes. Moreover, he found that Downes could and would assume responsibilities by Going the Extra Mile. What a pity that all of the

American people do not catch something of this spirit of assuming greater responsibilities. What a pity that more of us do not begin speaking more of our "privileges" of service under the American way of life, and less of the lack of opportunities in America.

Is there a man living in America today who would seriously claim that Carroll Downes would have been better off if he had been forced, by law or by group rule, to join the mad rush and quit his work at 5:30 in the afternoon? If he had done so, he would have received the standard wages for the sort of work he performed, but nothing more. Why should he receive more?

His destiny was in his own hands. It was wrapped up in this one lone privilege which should be the privilege of every American citizen: the right of personal initiative through the exercise of which he made it a habit always to Go the Extra Mile. That tells the whole story. There is no other secret to Downes' success. He admits it and everyone familiar with the circumstances of his promotion from poverty to riches knows it.

There is one thing no one seems to know: Why are there so few men who, like Carroll Downes, discover the power back of this business of doing more than one is paid for? It has in it the seed of all great achievement. It is the secret of all noteworthy success, and yet it is so little understood that most people look upon it as some clever trick with which employers try to get more work out of men.

This spirit of indifference toward the habit of Going the Extra Mile was dramatically expressed by a "wiseacre" who once applied to Henry Ford for a job. Mr. Ford questioned the man about his experience, his habits, and other routine matters, and was satisfied. Then he asked, "How much money do you want for your services?" The man was evasive on this point, so Mr. Ford finally said, "Well suppose you start in and show us what you can do, and we will pay you all you are worth after we have tried you out." He declined and explained, "I'm getting more than that where I am now employed." And I doubt not that he told the truth.

That explains precisely why so many people do not get ahead in life. They are "getting more than they are worth" where they are, and they seem never to learn how to get ahead by becoming worth more!

Just after the end of the Spanish-American War, Elbert Hubbard wrote a story entitled "A Message to Garcia." He told briefly how

President William McKinley commissioned a young soldier by the name of Rowan to carry a message from the United States Government to Garcia, the Cuban rebel chieftain, whose exact whereabouts were not known. This young soldier took the message, made his way through the vastness of the Cuban jungle, finally found Garcia, and delivered the note to him. That was all there was to the story—just a private soldier carrying out his orders under difficulties and getting the job done without coming back with an excuse.

The story fired imaginations all over the world. The simple act of a man doing what he was told and doing it well became news of the first magnitude. "A Message to Garcia" was printed in booklet form and sales reached an all-time high for such publications, amounting to more than ten million copies. This one story made Elbert Hubbard famous, to say nothing of helping to make him rich.

The story was translated into several foreign languages. The Japanese Government had it printed and distributed to every Japanese soldier. The Pennsylvania Railroad Company presented a copy of it to each of its thousands of employees. The big life insurance companies of America presented it to their salesmen. Long after Elbert Hubbard went down on the ill-fated Lusitania in 1915, "A Message to Garcia" continued as a best-seller throughout America.

The story was popular because it had in it something of the magic power that belongs to the man who does something and does it well.

The whole world is clamouring for such men. They are needed and wanted in every walk of life. American industry has always had princely berths for men who can and will assume responsibilities and get the thing done in the right "mental attitude" by Going the Extra Mile.

Andrew Carnegie lifted no fewer than forty such men from the lowly station of day labourers to that of millionaires. He understood the value of men who were willing to Go the Extra Mile.

Wherever he found such a man, he brought "his find" into the inner circle of his business and gave him an opportunity to earn "all he was worth."

Charles M. Schwab was one of those who gained the favour of the steel master by the simple expedient of Going the Extra Mile. He began work with Carnegie in the humble capacity of a stake driver at day wages. Step by step he climbed to the top and became Carnegie's right-hand man. Some years his income amounted to more than a million dollars in extra pay, in the form of a bonus.

The bonus was his compensation for Going the Extra Mile! His other pay was for the actual work he performed. Let us not forget that the "big money" is always the result, directly or indirectly, of that extra mile!

America is now passing through a great national crisis which seriously threatens the personal liberty which has made it possible for persons in all walks of life to Go the Extra Mile by exercising their own initiative.

The chief cause of this crisis has been the widespread endeavour of the people to get something for nothing, in direct opposition to the principle of Going the Extra Mile.

Human greed has taken the place of the desire to extend human kindness through useful service. The principle is exactly opposite to a demand for more pay and less work. Thousands have injured themselves by depending on public relief and substituting it for private initiative. The outlook of the future of the United States is indeed discouraging. Despite this handicap, I believe there are still enough people left in this country who are blessed with the common sense to stand up and speak out until the American people become aware of the abyss of self-destruction over which they are hanging.

People do things or refrain from doing them because of a motive. The soundest of motives for the habit of Going the Extra Mile is the fact that it yields enduring dividends in ways too numerous for mention, to all who follow the habit.

Americans want greater individual shares of the vast resources of this country. That is a healthy desire. The wealth is here in abundance, but let us stop this foolish attempt to get it the wrong way. Let us get our wealth by giving something of value in return for it. That is how Andrew Carnegie, Thomas A. Edison, Henry Ford, and many others of their type got theirs.

We know what are the rules by which success is attained. Let us appropriate these rules and use them intelligently, thereby acquiring the personal riches we demand, and adding to the wealth of the nation as well.

Some will say, "I am already doing more than I am paid for, but my employer is so selfish and greedy he will not recognize the sort of service I am rendering." We all know there are greedy men who want something for nothing; at least they want more than they earn. Selfish employers are like pieces of clay in the hands of a potter.

Through their greed they can be induced to reward the man who renders them more service than is paid for. Greedy employers do not wish to lose the services of one who makes a habit of Going the Extra Mile. They know the value of such employees. Here, then, is the crowbar and the fulcrum with which employers can be pried loose from their greed. Any clever man will know how to use this crowbar, not by withholding the quality or the quantity of the service he renders, but by increasing it.

I have seen this technique applied at least a hundred times, as a means of manipulating greedy employers through the recognition and use of their own weakness. On some occasions the employer failed to move as quickly as expected but that proved to be his hard luck, because his employee attracted the attention of a competitive employer who made a bid for his services and got them.

There is no way to cheat the man who follows the habit of Going the Extra Mile. If he does not get the proper recognition from one source, it comes voluntarily from some other source, generally when he least expects it. It always does come if one does more than he is paid for.

The man who Goes the Extra Mile and does it in the right sort of "mental attitude" never spends much time looking for a job. He doesn't have to, for the job is always looking for him. Depressions may come and go; business may be good or poor, the country may be at war or peace: but the man who renders more service and better service than he is paid for becomes indispensable to someone and thereby ensures himself against unemployment. The fallacy in much of our social security program is in the fact that it too frequently ignores the principle of the extra mile. It is based upon selfish protection by law.

High wages and indispensability are twin sisters. They always have been and they always will be!

The man who is smart enough to make himself indispensable to someone is smart enough to keep himself continuously employed, and at wages which are far greater than those coerced by group demands.

Henry Ford understands the value of indispensability. He also knows the value of Going the Extra Mile.

That is why some years ago he voluntarily raised the wages of his workers to an all-time high minimum daily wage of five dollars per day. By that act he did for his employees something that no labour leader could have forced him to do, and it was a smart move because it ensured him the sympathy and cooperation of his workers for more than a quarter of a century.

Andrew Carnegie understood the value of Going the Extra Mile. By putting that rule to work, he piled up a fortune of more than half a billion dollars. By some he was accused of being greedy, but he was never accused of being weak in the management of men. If he were greedy, he made wise use of his deficiency by paying some of his men (those who had the good sense to make themselves indispensable to him, by Going the Extra Mile) as much as a million dollars a year in extra bonuses. His policy was that of encouraging men to become indispensable to him by doing more than they were paid for (a privilege that was always available to his humblest worker), and then ensuring himself against their setting themselves up as rivals in business by paying them all they were actually worth.

By their recognition of the principle of Going the Extra Mile, these great men added many billions of dollars of additional wealth to the nation, provided profitable employment to many millions of men (employment that continued all through the depression), and piled up huge fortunes for their own use.

There has never been a time during the entire history of the United States when one could have benefited by the habit of doing more than paid for as he can today. The very fact that so many people are endeavouring to get something for nothing provides an unprecedented opportunity for those who refuse to yield to this common weakness. These few may profit by the law of contrast, by adopting and applying the habit of Going the Extra Mile.

Readers should grasp the full meaning of the principle of Going the Extra Mile, and make the most of it now, in this hour of national emergency when one's loyalty to his country can best be demonstrated by useful service. The present emergency threatens to destroy the very institution which makes it possible for men to promote themselves by rendering superior service. Therefore, it is not only a profitable privilege to go the extra mile, but it is absolutely essential that we do so. The principle of the extra mile is typical of and vital to democracy.

Our country still is a "land of opportunity", for every man who is willing to render useful service in return for the better things of life. Our country can remain "the cradle of human liberty and freedom", only as long as we deserve this privilege, by rendering useful service in a spirit of unselfishness.

There comes a time in the history of every nation when its people must put aside greed and selfishness and work for the common good of one another or perish. Throughout the world people today are forced to meet the challenge of brute force and human greed for power! Whenever such emergencies have arisen in this country, the people have met them successfully by putting aside selfishness and voluntarily Going the Extra Mile.

There is a definite reason why our country is known as the "richest and the freest" country. That reason has its roots in the efficiency of the men who have pioneered in the organization of our industrial and economic development.

Industry, which is the major foundation stone of Americanism, has thrived because of the great army of far-sighted men who have made it their business to do more than they were paid for. These leaders have accumulated riches in abundance; but their riches have been used in a manner that has provided employment for a vast majority of those who work for wages. Therefore, their individual wealth has become a part of the national wealth of this country.

Take Henry Ford, for example. He has accumulated a great fortune, but who would deny that this country would be better off today if it could boast of a thousand such men, each of whom provided employment to millions of men, as Mr. Ford has done? It is estimated that directly and indirectly Henry Ford provides employment for no fewer than 6,000,000 men. His influence on the American way of life is beyond estimate, but we do know that he has been largely responsible for the network of improved highways which make every portion of the country easily accessible by dependable, rapid transportation. The taxes collected annually by both state and federal governments because of Mr. Ford's industry are beyond estimate.

Henry Ford's success has not been accidental. It is the result of definite rules of procedure. We know the nature of these rules, one of the most prominent of which is that of Going the Extra Mile.

The author has been guided by a strict adherence to the discoveries of science and the laws of nature. Nowhere in the entire field of science do we find any justification for regulatory laws that discourage men from using their personal initiative to the fullest extent possible, but we do find definite justification of the habit of Going the Extra Mile. That justification consists in the fact that nowhere at any time have we found a successful industry, or a successful individual, who did not practice this principle. On the other hand, we have examined thousands of instances in connection with which individuals met with defeat and went down in many forms of personal and business failure by neglecting or refusing to Go the Extra Mile.

It is a well-known fact that men of science and men of education reach conclusions and create plans by the safe method of learning from the experiences of men of established authority in their respective fields of individual endeavour. The purpose of the great libraries of the country is mainly that of providing all the people with a record of the knowledge that civilization has sifted from the experiences of people. Men who think, men who are successful, make it their business to learn, through systematic research into these records of past experiences, all that has been recorded in connection with their own interests in life. The man who neglects or refuses to find out what others in his chosen field of endeavour have learned which may be of use to him, overlooks a great privilege.

> The Depression taught us that there is something worse than being forced to work. It is being forced not to work.

Before this philosophy in this chapter was completed more than twenty years of painstaking research was devoted to the study of the records of men who have been recognized as the ablest thinkers and philosophers the world has known. A staff of intelligent research specialists were kept busy, and they combed the libraries for authentic records of the experiences of men who have been recognized as the leaders in almost every field of human endeavour. The substance of their findings was written into this philosophy. In addition to this form of research into the history of the experiences of men, more than 500 of the most successful men known to the American people collaborated over a long period of years by providing the essence of the knowledge they had gathered from the trial-and-error system in the field of industry and business. Moreover, a careful personal analysis was made of thousands of men and women in all walks of life, representing a cross-section of the American people and the American way of life, from which the author uncovered the causes of failure as well as the causes of success. From the findings of this extensive research, this philosophy was organized.

So, when I present the readers with a clearly marked road map that leads to individual achievement, they may be assured that the map was drawn from the footprints of men who have travelled that road before them.

Application of the principles of Going the Extra Mile, Definiteness of Purpose, and the Mastermind Group are the sure way to find the Path to Personal Power.

□□□